DAY TRADING FOR BEGINNERS:

Tips and Strategies to Earn Online in Futures with Psychology secrets. Cryptocurrency, Forex, Stocks Market to Make a Living and Create a Passive Income from Home.

II

Introduction *1*

Chapter 1: How to Start Day Trading *4*

Chapter 2: Trading Platforms *17*

Chapter 3: Selecting a Broker *21*

Chapter 4: Day Trading Orders *29*

Chapter 5: Most Important Day Trading Strategies
.... *53*

Chapter 6: Trading and Time *57*

Chapter 7: What Should You Invest in to Be Profitable at Day Trading *63*

Chapter 8: From Mere Income Generation to Vocation *77*

Chapter 9: Momentum Trading *81*

Chapter 10: Deflation vs. Inflation How to Fight Them *95*

Chapter 11: Portfolio Diversification *99*

Chapter 12: Money Management *117*

Chapter 13: Risk Management Strategies *143*

Conclusion *151*

Introduction

Futures are agreements created to either purchase or sell a particular security at a later date and at specific prices. Futures are normally traded on an exchange similar to stocks and options. An individual commit to purchasing a certain amount of securities or assets, and the seller undertakes to deliver the same at a future date. People who engage in trading futures include investors, companies as well as speculators.

Just like options, futures represent derivatives of an underlying stock. This means that the price of a futures contract changes depending on changes in the underlying instrument. The process of day trading futures is different from trading stocks because when trading futures, you do not get to own the shares associated with the lying instrument.

There are several reasons why people engage in day trading using futures. Some of these include:

- *Low prices* – when day trading stocks, the capital requirements are too high. However, you do not need a lot of capital to trade in futures. You can start trading with as low as $5000, or less depending on the trading platform.
- **Price changes with the underlying security – *the amount of profit you make from day trading futures is determined by the price***

changes in the underlying security. This implies that you can use technical analysis strategies to leverage the income you receive from trading futures.

- *No short-selling restrictions* – short-term traders often depend on each trade to realize some good profits. When trading futures, there are no restrictions on both long and short trading positions. This means that you can apply market analysis information on all kinds of futures. This is not the case with stock day trading since you must have stock in place before selling it at a profit. This restriction makes it impossible for you to short-sell when trading stocks.

To start day trading futures, you need a few tools and resources similar to those required when selling stocks. There are minimum capital regulations to be met, and you must also work through a broker. Once you identify a broker, you will need to select the kind of futures contract you wish to trade. When doing this, there are several factors that you must consider including the volume of trade and previous price movement of the futures contract, among others.

There are several risks involved in day trading futures as well. Most traders always borrow capital to invest in the futures market because of the substantial profit margins involved. Small price changes still result in exponentially significant returns. However, trading in futures using borrowed money always results in high risk. If the market direction does not assume the expected direction, you will end up losing the borrowed money. Futures possess a high leverage potential that traders take advantage of. This leverage presents a high-profit potential, but also creates a platform for more significant loss.

Chapter 1: How to Start Day Trading

Day trading is becoming a lucrative engagement in the commerce industry with recent technological advancement. Hey there, welcome to the stock market world. This end is strategically oriented and plenty of fat risks coming your way. Let's dive into some of the factors that are likely to be considered.

The Capital Needed to Start Day Trading

Capital is so necessary to set the actual day trading ball on fire. Acquiring loans from different sites has been revealed to be so common among traders. With this glue on the mind, traders tend to be so careful with the amount of capital that they actually intend to commence with. To begin, traders are ought to obtain ready capital so as to monitor any kind of slight changes that are presumed to occur during the course of the day.

Day trading requires a minimum account balance of $1000, but $8000-$10,000 is recommended by many providers and plenty of traders are not willing to risk 1% from the value. Also, the $1000 minimum amount that can be implemented can lead to your trading activities in being so not worthwhile.

Step by step kind of beginning is so vital because you get to acquire progress constantly and get to grow at a good speed with messing things out.

Choosing a Broker

Once you have set your mind on exactly what intend to trade, a broker should be following up in mind. Brokers are the navigators of several trading investment platforms. Bearing this I mind, we ought to be super perfect in choosing a broker because they reflect reliability, reputations, and expertise in your trading account.

Let us look at some of the ways that are set to be considered:
- ☐ Really decide on what you will be trading.

Experts get their names by being good (perfect) in a particular field of trading. A stocks broker may be so bad in FOREX trading and vice versa. All the best in picking the best and the right one.

- ☐ Sourcing for recommendations.

Sticking in mind that the actual amount of money to be used during trading is really your own money, a wake-up call is assured and a good broker who can't be dodging with your precious money is super needed.

Try to even inquire from your colleagues you may have been in the previous spot or who they may have heard of good brokers.

Try to also have some in-depth research from varieties of social media content, online reviews on the investment platforms, discussion boards and also take plenty of time to examine their websites.

Once you get several references, don't hesitate to check on their trading platforms. How were their actions? Any available complaints? How many traders have they ever been engaged with? How long have they been doing this? Have they been following the rules and regulations needed as a broker?

☐   Commissions rate.

Despite the fact that the "perfect" broker is super needed as you begin day trading, consider in mind that this is also a new project as a whole. Meaning that profits too, need to be made so as this whole project can exist for a long while. Consider the rates of commissions that are likely to be spent so as to avoid any losses from being made. Pick an economical one so as to really save yourself.

☐   Executive Speed.

Any delay of seconds can result in a massacre to a trader's profits. To prevent this, the broker should really make sure that the trading activities are at a top-notch. The broker should be able to quickly spot any rapid changes that are likely to be incurred in the trading platforms.

☐   Charting strategies.

Getting great chatting tools and software is also fundamental. Make sure you are getting good trading strategies, reliable variable markets, and better software features to enhance good day trading

☐ Paper trading.

It's advisable to begin day trading with paper trading, where you won't have to use your own money, though many brokers highly discourage this. Know where your heart takes you.

☐ Technology.

So, is the broker up for the new technological advancements? What kinds of accounts do they deal with? Does he/she have a real-time-data feed so that you can easily track and monitor trading activities? Which safeguard trading and Cybersecurity measures do they follow during trading? What kind of volumes of trading can they handle?

Greatly consider the kind who's so updated with the current technological happenings and pretty much informed.

☐ Customer service provision.

Are they willing to offer customer service services? What happens when your system during mid-trade and it costs you so much? Are they going to support you so as to get much out of trading? Which process are they going to utilize during complaint resolution? And many more. Consider these before signing the contract because it's a big deal.

☐ Safe, secure and regulated.

It's such a marvelous idea to inquire about the security of the broker in question. Inquire on how long they have been in business, their past work reports, what measures they have been using and their recent big measures on day trading.

Make sure they regulated by an agency and that they strictly value and consider the rules and regulations needed to be followed by any broker engaged in day trading.

- Adequate support.

Engage with brokers that are willing to provide huge support once there is a miss during your daily training activities. A few cents incremented on the broker's commission accounts is much worthwhile compared to hundreds of dollars losses that are likely to be incurred on the bad days.

How to Become a Day Trader

The following basic tools are recommended:

Computer/Monitor.

Well, cheap is expensive. A slow kind of computer can cause you a great fortune. Slow working definitely implies that the day trading tracks to be unreliable and totally not trending. This is really going to cost you in that the rates of profits at the end of any activity will be way low. They can cause you to miss trades, therefore, making your idea so unreliable. Remember you have a good reputation to uphold.

With all these in mind, please bear a quite fast laptop or monitor.

Set a target, really motivating.

Setting a realistic trading target is going to manage and monitor your real cash big time. A certain target is put for the purpose of big motivation. Work on that. Be for it big time. Remember achieving your target is normally tough because we all have really "dream" targets. Consistent losses will be incurred too, so prepare to lose some cash. Failure is never good though and will never be, So keep up champ!

Create a demo account.

Rehearsing has been always been a good move as your head to be successful navigation. Set up a demo account that will help you master all the ropes and moves that are likely to be incurred. Reading the fluctuations, the market trends are one way of future taking master moves that are great chances for high profitability rates. Keep testing and practicing until you are sure that you indeed set to go. Examine the market.

Master most of the trading moves. This makes you informed and definitely enhances specialization in a particular field.

Fast internet connection.

A constant, fast and reliable type of internet connection is highly recommended. The unreliable internet connection can cause a miss in the market trends that can hinder the trading traces in a way leading to major losses being incurred at the end. Most of the users use a cable and ADSL type of connection. Remember that day trading does not recommend any unreliable source of connection.

Type of market.

As discussed earlier, each kind of day trading demands a different kind of day trading. Choosing the kind of market to start with is super important, choose the most preferred.

Discover the tax implications likely to be incurred.

Inquire on how taxes revolve around profits. Engage with your financial adviser to let him or her explain how taxes are handled. Are they going to cause a devaluation on the made profits? Are they good news? How does that happen?

Be informed so as to at the end the trader can guess on the likelihood net profits to be expected.

Choose the right stocks to trade.

Well, to be better in choosing the right kind of stock, doing some in-depth research on the current existing stock is way the first step. Get to know the kind of stocks that are likely to perform well. Most preferably, those that are likely to perform well on a day-to-day basis. Remember to at least try one or two different kinds of stock until you are so sure that you have picked out the right one.

Plan a good financial figure.

You will need to prepare yourself early enough on the amount of money that can be risked on the day trading business. It is mostly advised not to risk more than 1-2% of your account money so as to avoid future losses.

Another piece of advice to the beginners, stay away from trading on the margin until you are set with enough moves and good trading wisdom. This will save you some extra cash in time.

Know the lingo.

Becoming an expert clearly requires much effort. There are certain keywords that you are required to be familiar with. Check them out:

- Ask the amount of money a trader is offering for sale.
- Know the bid: This is the money amount a trader is ready to purchase.
- Stock breakouts: Declaring a stock that has experienced a breakout, basically talks of its reduction in the level of resistance.
- Candlestick: This is a type of chart specifically for prices that shows the maximum, minimum, opening and closing prices for a specified period of time.
- Covering: This refers to the buying back of the trade shares that had been sold earlier to do away with the obligation.
- Float: This is the amount of market share that is ready for day trading.
- Stock Gap Up or Down: This normally occurs when the price of a market trade becomes more or less than its previous closing price.
- The idea of Going Long: This normally refers to buying a market trade with the objective of offering it for sale at a higher price.

- High of Day and Low of Day: This is the highest or the lowest price a market trade has traded throughout the day.

- Hard to borrow list: This is ideally a list used by brokers that tells the stocks that are hard to borrow for short term sales.

- Market liquidity: This is a term that describes the state of the market showing how fast an inventory can be sold or purchased without affecting its price.

- Low Float Stock: This is basically a type of stock with a low number of shares available for trading.

- Market Maker: This term generally refers to any market participant, be it a firm or an individual who can purchase, sell and clear market trades. A market maker normally operates under given by-laws of a country.

- Market Capitalization: This refers to the overall value of shares and stock of a business center. Most specifically ordinary shares (unit of capital).

- Outstanding Shares: This is a type of shares that have been given out by a company and have been subscribed by shareholders. They are normally shown as share capital in the company's balance sheet.

- The P&L (Profits and Losses): This is a financial statement, also referred to as an income statement. It indicates the revenue, costs, and expenses incurred by a business for a specified period of time normally a quarter a year.
- Red Green trading: The red and green colors on trading charts also have meaning. The green bar indicates the stock which is higher compared to the previous day. The red bar scenario shows the stock which closed lower that day as compared with the previous day.
- Resistance: This is the price point of stock which is normally at a higher level. The price level overpowers buyers, making it hard for the inventory to have a price increase.
- Scalping: Considering every small price ranges that are likely to happen during day trading.
- Short Selling: This activity involves selling off some shares at a price that is likely to make a good profit when buying them later.
- Spread: This is the price bridge between the bid and asks during day trading.
- Support trading. This is a section in a trading chart that indicates where price had dropped and tried it best to break below.

- Technical Analysis: Historical analysis of the price of the stock is involved with the use of mechanisms like charts so as to predict possible outcomes in the future.

- Top trends: This is an actual graphical representation of the stock's movement within trading while monitoring the top trends and downtrends. Trends are so important in day trading because they give the brokers and traders a sense of a particular direction and makes them informed of all moves and plan for better strategies.

Chapter 2: Trading Platforms

If you are an experienced trader and you want to take a chance at taking on the market, you probably know what you want in a brokerage like comprehensive trading platforms, innovative strategy tools, premium research, and low costs. We have chosen some of the best brokers that you can use only in several different categories, so you will be able to choose one that is based on your personal priorities.

These next brokers have great pricing over their competitors and they have great trading tools and platforms:

Interactive Brokers and OptionsHouse have a powerful combination that each trader wants: Advanced trading tools and platforms paired with low commissions. Interactive Brokers tend to be the choice of traders that like per share pricing and is able to meet a minimum account of $10,000 with a minimum monthly commission of $10. This slightly affects their rating. OptionsHouse, on the other hand, gives traders a flat rate, and they don't require a minimum balance. The downside is they don't have forex trading. Interactive Brokers gives you access to forex, futures, and precious metals.

These brokers offer the most powerful platforms that are available without any fees or minimums:

OptionsHouse and Interactive Brokers have powerful platforms. Charles Schwab and TD Ameritrade also surpass others. TD Ameritrade probably has the best platform out there, thinkorswim, as well as Trade Architect that is very simple to use. Charles Schwab also gives you two great platforms: Streetsamrt.com is a great platform for beginners. StreetSmart Edge is a more advanced functionality in charting. Both of which can be used by traders and they don't require any balance or activity minimums. Remember that there is an avoidable account minimum account balance of $1,000.

These brokers offer powerful tools and competitive pricing for options traders:

TradeStation and OptionsXpress are two more great options for traders to use. Which one you like the best will depend on what you are looking for in trade activity and platform needs. TradeStation is aimed more towards the professional trader. This platform will cost $99.95 each month, which is waived if you trade at least 5,000 shares, ten futures options or round-turn futures contracts, 50 options contracts, or carried a $100,000 balance. TradeStation's pricing is favorable to bulk traders, which give per-contract, flat fees, or volume discounts. OptionsXpress don't require trade or account balance minimums, carry the extra fees, or offers competitive commissions, and they don't have vigorous trading. Trades with OptionsXpress only cost $1.25 for each contract for traders who are active, and they have a $12.95 minimum charge for ten or fewer contracts

Traders that utilize margin needs to prioritize broker's margin rates while they search. These online brokers have the lowest margin rates:

None of the others can even come close to Interactive Brokers when you look at their margin rates. If margin rates are your priority, then this is a good option for you. This broker will charge you a grouped rate that is based on the balance of your account but also has a calculator to help traders to perform their math quicker. Interactive Brokers do have a minimum of monthly trade. EOption's deposit requirement is a lot lower, and they have a more reasonable trade requirement. They only charge a $50 inactivity fee when you don't trade at least two times a year or who has less than $100,000 in debit or credit balances. Both of these options have competitive commissions for their options and stock trades.

Chapter 3:
Selecting a Broker

Who Is A Broker?

This is someone who buys and sells goods or things on behalf of someone else. They mostly are middle men in transactions, that often they make profit out of. They only have to organize and plan for transactions to take place between a purchaser/buyer and a vendor/seller. The broker ends up getting a commission out of the deal, either from the buyer or seller. Most of the time they represent the seller.

Brokers may be individuals or firms. When it is a firm, it still acts as a go between their customer and the vendor.

Brokers exist in many different industries. An example would be real estate brokers who advertise and sell properties on behalf of the owners. We also have insurance brokers who sell insurance on behalf of firms. We have stock market brokers who work on the stock market.

Why Use A Broker?

There are a few advantages of using brokers in any kind of business. As usual, before getting into any business with a broker, always do intensive research on what you are about to get into. There are a few bad crops in the market.

1. They know their market well

Most brokers are people or firms who have been in the field for quite a while and always know what is best for one client to the other. They also know who to talk to if you need anything specific and always do it well knowing they will benefit.

Brokers have been on the market for a long time and have seen what goes on and know too well what to expect. They have all the information you need right from the time you enter the market to the time you leave. They are particularly important when you are entering a foreign market that you aren't familiar with. You need to take time and look for the perfect broker that will tell you what you need and how to do things the right way. However, you need to be wary of the brokers who are out to exploit you. Use referrals and other methods to try and get the right broker who understands your needs.

2. Wider representation

A client is able to reach more people or a wide marker when using a broker, compared to them doing it by themselves. Brokers are also quite affordable, and have a network they work with; hence there is limited cost incurrence with them. Because most of them are well known, they are able to reach a wider market ratio easily.

When you decide to work with a broker, you get to cast your net wider so that you can get better business. Coming up with a network takes time, which is why it is just right that you work with a person that already has a network which you can tap in. This saves you time and effort, as well as money. Take time to work with a broker that already has a network of established clients.

3. Special skills and knowledge

Brokers mostly have special knowledge of the field they are in and are good at the specific brokerage area. This is because they work in detail so as to know the needs of different types of clients. Because of this, they are an asset to anyone who is looking for their services.

The skills that a broker has vary from customer relationship management to money management. They will help you to grow your empire as you sit and wait for them to do the work you want. It takes experience and a lot of patience for you to learn the skills and be able to do the things that a broker can do. So, always make use of a broker when making trading decisions.

4. Customer choice

Brokers always work with the customer's choice. They will always want to know what one needs they will always endeavor to ensure the customer is satisfied and has what they originally wanted, or better.

5. Time saving

Because they mostly know their trade well, a broker would be able to achieve more within a shorter period of time for the customer. This is because of their great networking within their field of specialization. They always know where to find what, at what time and for what amount.

The time that you save when you work with a broker can be used to handle other tasks that you have. Take time to make sure the broker knows what they are doing otherwise you will end up wasting a lot of time.

Types of Brokers

- *Stock broker*
- *Business broker*
- *Pawn Broker*
- *Information broker*
- *Insurance broker*
- *Investment broker*

Roles Played by Brokers in Forex Trading

For a long while, people have been quite skeptical about the Forex market, but this is something that has been growing rapidly the last few years. Forex trading has become one of the leading markets in the trading world. It generally involves the process of changing one currency to another for certain reasons. Currencies trade against each other depending on the exchange rates and brokers use the growth on these rates to make profits. Because of this, there has been a high need of Forex brokers who are the middle men for investors who want to invest in Forex. Forex brokers are usually people or firms that provide currency traders with a platform to buy and sell their currency. They end up controlling a small portion of the large Forex market.

Their importance varies from need basis:

1. Link between the trader and the market

There are many investors who have a lot of funds and want to grow their wealth in Forex trading, but have no idea how to go about it. This is where brokers come in, and act as their representatives in the Forex market. Brokers know all the nooks and crooks of Forex trading, and always know when to take advantage of the exchange rate changes. They are best placed to give advice on how to go about trading, as they are always doing it as a day job hence very experienced.

Brokers always know when to take advantage of the market and the different events that would lead to an increase or decrease in the exchange rate, and hence know when to make the right moves. This they do at a smaller fee, so their aim is to have as many clients as possible so they can thrive on numbers.

2. Help educate investors or other beginner brokers

Brokers have lots of information on trading than most people would, and it is advisable for any beginner to have one to share tips with them. They would know how to go about avoiding some basic mistakes people make when they start investing in Forex markets.

3. They trade and negotiate on behalf of investors

Brokers are mostly the same as sales representatives. They trade currencies online, and the skilled ones do it as a daily job hence very useful for any beginner investor.

There are very many investors who want to trade but have no time, hence use brokers who do it full time. The Forex market is a 24-hour business operation and the exchange rates tend to rise and drop every moment. This means anyone trading has to always be on standby to make a move. Brokers do this on behalf of other people who have the money to invest but have no time. This as times is most ideal as the brokers always know the right moves that bring in profits and incase of losses, they always know the move to make to reduce the amount of losses made.

4. Advise traders on risks that come with Forex trading

Forex trading, just like any other trading in the stock market, is a risky affair. As it highly involves currency values, there are times that the fluctuations can affect the market and a broker should be keen enough to know the right move to make.

Every investment has pros and cons, which are risks that investors will encounter one way or the other. One might lose more than the value of their transaction, but with a skilled broker to guide you through, you might be able to salvage the situation.

Major risk factors one might encounter:

Exchange rate risk: this is the risk that comes by as a result of changes in the value of the currency. There is a constant shift on the worldwide supply and demand balance, which might end up affecting the traders' position. This mostly depends on whichever way the currencies will move based on different factors. It is in this case where a broker advises one to cut losses early enough by taking different positions. These could be the position limit or loss limit. Other risks include:

- *Interest rate risk*
- Credit risk
- Country risk
- Liquidity risk
- Transactional risk
- Risk of ruin

5. Customer support during local trading hours

6. Ideas on latest trading platforms

Before you can work with a broker, you need to choose one. Choosing a broker isn't an easy task at all because you have hundreds of brokers to choose from. The best thing to do in this case is to try and make sure you work with referrals and testimonials when making a decision. Based on facts when getting the right broker.

Chapter 4:
Day Trading Orders

Stock trading involves a lot more than selling and buying of assets and securities. There are several orders used in each technique of trading. Each order is created to fulfill a particular task on the market. Let us look at some of the orders you can employ in day trading and how you can use them.

- *Market Order is* one of the easiest orders to raise. It can be divided into two – market orders for buying and market orders for selling. This order provides you information about the market price. For instance, if you create a market order to purchase a particular asset or derivative. You will be able to see a list of all the sellers on the market plus the price of their securities. If you raise an order to sell, you will gain access to a list of available buyers together with their bid prices. Day traders use market orders to enter or exit trades faster, especially when the prices are changing drastically.

The disadvantage of market orders, though, is that you can never tell the exact opening or closing price of a transaction. The prices always depend on the volume of the stock you decide to trade in.

- *Buy stop order* is placed by day traders seeking to purchase stocks at a price that is higher than the current price. The order is filled when the price goes above the indicated stop price. The order is mostly used to restrict losses incurred on a short trade position when the market prices start moving in an unfavorable direction.

- *Sell stop order* is utilized when the price drops below the current stock price. When you raise this order, it can only be filled when the stop price is higher or the same as the current stock price. Day traders use this kind of order to exit long trades that have assumed a losing direction.

- *Buy limit order* is placed when the day trader wishes to purchase at a cost that is lower than the current stock price. This gives you an opportunity to control the amount of cash you pay for a particular purchase position. When you create a buy limit order, you can only buy the stock at the current price or lower, not higher. One disadvantage of this kind of order is that you are never sure if it will be filled. If the amount of stock keeps going higher than the current price, then you will not succeed in purchasing any stock.

- *Sell limit order* is the opposite of the buy limit order. When you raise this order, you are indicating a willingness to sell a security or asset at a price that is higher than the current stock price. Like the buy limit order, you can only fill this order if the price rises above the current price. The aim of using this order is to make you generate profit from any long trades that you engage in.

- *Buy stop limit order* works the same way as the buy stop order, only that is works differently from the market order. This order gets completed when the price of the stock reaches the buy stop limit amount or less. It prevents you from paying more than the anticipated amount for each trade thus reducing the number of losses you may incur

- *Sell stop limit order* - sell stop limit order also plays the same role as the sell stop order but does not mimic the market order. When you place this kind of order, it only gets filled when the stock price attains an amount that is equal or more than the stop limit price. Setting the wrong order for your day trading activities can cause you to end into problems. The more you practice how to use the orders, the more you will understand how and when to apply them.

What Day Traders Do Every day

A typical day in the life of the day trader is often filled with lots of exciting activities. What the trader spends time doing during the day determines the amount of profit he makes at the end of the day. Some of the days are always smooth and less busy while others involve a lot of activities.

Traders rise early enough to study the market as they prepare for the day. Depending on one's location, morning hours may present some excellent trading opportunities or some not so good ones. Day traders always take advantage of this period because the prices are the most liquid, and the most volatile. Here are some of the primary stages a day trader goes through each day

1. *Preparing for the day*

Day traders always take time to prepare for the day as a way of ensuring that things go as planned during the entire day. Some ensure that they get up at least an hour before the trading session begins. This is in order to:

- Go through the necessary strategies for the day and resolve any issues faced the previous day

- Create a trading plan for the day or revise existing plans accordingly

- Adjust account balances accordingly and determine how much they are ready to risk losing that day

- Check any changes in price and financial news that can affect market direction

- Analyze the trading platform to ensure it's still working well

2. Trading Session

Day traders always make transactions the first few hours after the market opens. Depending on how active the market is, some opt to trade for more extended periods, until most of the stocks become less volatile.

Although beginners in the trade always think that they have to spend a lot of time online to make a profit, this is not the case. Professional day traders only visit the trading platforms to enter or exit positions and set the necessary orders for the day. Once some orders are filled, trades associated with such orders always close automatically. This means that you do not need to spend all your time on day trading platforms to make a profit.

3. *Review*

Takes place at the end of the trading day. For some, the day can end as early as 11:00 am while for others; it may end as late as 6:00 pm. At this point, the trader goes through the day's business and notes down every activity and results of each trade. This is where the trader also calculates the profits or losses incurred and notes down what needs to be done to improve future trading experiences. A basic review always consists of the number of hours spent on the trading platform and the number of positions completed successfully. It also consists of the number of successful or unsuccessful trades as well as the net profit or loss.

Without the right plan and strategy, day trading becomes a less exciting venture. However, traders who have mastered the necessary moves on the market always enjoy every bit of the business. The secret to becoming better at the trade lies in doing a lot of practice.

Trading Goals for Overcoming Constraints

Trading goals are different from ordinary goals. The main purpose for each trader is always to make a profit from each trade. However, day trading goals go beyond basic selling and buying of stocks at a profit. Several attributes define achievable day trading goals:

- *They focus on the trading process and not the benefits.* You probably know that the main focus of creating goals is making them specific and measurable. In day trading, you must ensure that the goals you make do not focus on the amount of money you wish to build over time. You should instead concentrate on the efforts you need to put in the process you use. When the process is perfect, the results will automatically be positive

- *They are defense-minded.* If you set goals that are not defense-minded, you will end up pursuing trading opportunities only for the sake of financial gain. However, your goals should seek to protect your capital. Doing this will keep you into business even when you are not making any profit. You can do this by setting limit orders for each trading period. Also, you can outline a risk tolerance plan that indicates the amount you are willing to lose in every trade. With these figures in place, you can always customize your strategies and trading techniques to ensure that you do not exceed these limits.

- *They are progressive.* Sound goals allow you to get into the day trading business gradually. They ensure that you do not skip any step of the trading process and that you acquire the necessary training before jumping into the trade. You can do this by ensuring that you do not risk more than you are willing to lose. And that you do not depend on market indicators to make trading decisions all the time.

Setting clear, realistic goals is a must for every day trader. However, you must remember that your goals must never be profit-oriented. This is one grave mistake that most traders make. The right goals will always prevent you from over-risking your capital and overtrading.

Day Trading and Emotions

Day trading involves making quick decisions. This explains why you must always have your emotions under control. If you fail to control them, you may lose any profits and capital accumulated over time in a single trade gone wrong.

When most traders lose part of their capital to some trades, they tend to get frustrated and fearful. This causes them to overleverage the little money remaining. As a result, they end up blowing their account in one or a few risky trades. Day trading is not like other long-term trading strategies where you can quickly determine the direction of market prices. That is why you need to stick to your initial plan and strategy.

One of the attributes that make day traders remain in business is discipline. The strategy demands a lot of concentration and focus. You must, therefore, seek to understand how best to control your emotions when trading. Let us look at some of the things you need to do to avoid emotional trading:

- *Avoid less volatile trading seasons.* Most day traders prefer trading during sessions of high volatility. This sometimes leads to congestion in the marketplace, and if you do not have the right skills and strategies, you may end up frustrated. If the market gets flooded and the prices seem stagnant, avoid entering any positions as this can result in tremendous losses.

- *Exit the market after a few wins.* Once you make three or more consecutive wins, stop trading until another time. This also applies to losing. When you win consecutively, you may start feeling that you are a super trader. In such excitement, you can end up entering the wrong trades, thus losing all your profits. Most people revenge trade as a way of recovering what they have already lost. This results in more losses. Therefore, you should exit the market for a few minutes or hours when you consistently win or lose.

- *Take a break between trades.* Given the rapid changes in market prices when day trading, it is easy for you to get drowned into the trade and forget about your emotions. You must take a break from the trading platform after each trade. This will give you time to reflect on the next move you need to make and give you better control of your emotions.

- *Don't focus on the outcome.* To keep your emotions in check, avoid checking your losses and profits when trading. If you do this, you will definitely experience a surge of emotions that may be difficult to control. Always stick to the rules of trade as you hope to gain some profit at the end of the day.

As you do the above, you must bear in mind that controlling your emotions needs a lot of patience and perseverance. You must keep improving on your emotional stability for the long-term success of your business. With time, you will realize that you do not need to concentrate on managing any emotions. You would have rained your brain to respond to the various emotional triggers.

Factors to Consider When Starting Day Trading

To succeed in day trading, there are some few factors you need to put into consideration. Here are some of them.

1. The kind of security to trade. You cannot trade every commodity on the market. You must concentrate on specific products when day trading. When selecting a broker to work with, you will be expected to list the kind of instruments you want to trade in. Most day traders only engage in stock trading. However, there are several other instruments that you can focus on, such as derivatives, options, and futures.

2. Chose the right broker. Once you identify the kind of instrument to trade, it is also essential that you get the right broker for the instrument. Brokers are often interested in working with day traders because of the high commissions involved. You must be careful that you do not get one that doesn't have experience in this kind of trade. Check out for things like the commissions and margin rates charged to ensure that you remain with some good profits at the end of the day. Also, ensure that the broker offers the best research and trading tools.

3. Set trading sessions. Although day trading does not require that you stick to a particular routine, you can

identify specific times that work for you and stick to trading during these times. Most day traders enter the market during morning hours, or a few hours before the day ends. You can choose a time that suits your schedule.

4. Determine how much you can risk in the trade. This will ensure that you do not end up frustrated in case you lose part of your capital. It is always advisable that you risk 2% or less of your capital for each trade. You must set this time ahead of every trade to ensure that you do not exceed it. You also need to add any interest charges to this amount since most brokers charge a reasonable amount as interest.

Day Trading Stocks and the Strategies Involved

As stated earlier in this chapter, most day traders concentrate on trading stocks more than other financial instruments. Although stocks are considered as great investments for long-term traders, day traders can take advantage of the changes in stock prices to make some profit out of it. Multiple strategies are available for use by day traders who deal with stocks. One of these is scalping which focuses on generating several small profits from the small price changes that occur in the stock market. This strategy focuses on the number of trades, not the quality of trade. Another strategy is the use of moving average crossovers which allows you to make a purchase when a fast-moving average cross over a slow-moving one.

Day Trading Pros and Cons

Day trading has become quite popular among online traders in the recent past. With increased advancement in the stock trading industry, day trading has been identified as one of the profitable opportunities that you can engage in. Of course, the main reason why people choose a trading strategy over the other is the potentiality of the approach generating some good income. However, day trading has several better advantages over other trading strategies by far. These advantages are listed below.

Easy to learn – it is easy to learn and start day trading. In case you begin trading using penny stocks, you do not require a license or training to get started. All you need is an internet connection, a functional laptop, and some little capital. However, this becomes a drawback if you start trading without the necessary information. With proper preparation, you can get started without needing any assistance from other traders.

Better control of your capital - This is one of the most exciting aspects of day trading. You are always the determinant factor for your success. You control how your capital gets utilized and how you use the profits realized from the trade. The kind of strategies and plans you come up with determine how much you get at the end of each day. If you do not spend time seeking to understand how the strategy works, you may end up getting frustrated with the business. You are also responsible for determining your schedules. This means that you can do day trading at a time that is convenient for you so long as the market is still open for trading.

Succeeding is easy - One other advantage of day trading is that it has an explicit guarantee of success. This is because stock prices always keep fluctuating every day, meaning that there is always an opportunity to make money out of the business. So long as you are determined to make the right moves on the market, you can be sure of making some profit at the end of the day. Most of the required research is already done by the experts. All you need to do is apply the right types of orders and strategies at the right time.

Availability of Resources – several years ago, traders could pay financial institutions a lot of cash to gain access to market data and other trading resources. With the availability of the internet today, it is very easy to find free, educative resources about day trading online. There are tutorials, workshops, webinars, and free online courses that you can enroll in to gain more understanding of the strategy.

Quick profits - When compared to other trading strategies, day trading offers you a quick turnaround in terms of profit. You do not have to wait for extended periods to gain access to your money since it is made available to you at the end of each trading day. Although there are several risks involved in the trade, the reward potential is too significant to be realized. If you are seeking to make large profits within a short time, you may attempt day trading.

Overnight risks do not exist - In day trading; you close every trade position at the end of the trading day. This ensures that you do not risk your capital by holding onto stocks overnight. Markets change a lot during the night. Holding onto positions the entire night always results in an increased risk of losing your income. As you close the business at the end of each day, you are always sure that you will start afresh the following day without having to incur any more losses.

You can make profit from bad markets - Through the use of short selling and other favorable strategies, day traders can easily make some income from markets whose prices are on the decline. This is one of the most significant pros in day trading.

The use of technical analysis - Traders often uses fundamental and technical analysis to interpret financial market information. Long-term trading strategies always concentrate on using fundamental analysis to determine market prices. Day traders, on the other hand, can utilize technical analysis to determine what is happening on the market at the current moment. Doing this ensures that the traders understand the right time to enter or close positions as a way of making a profit from the business.

Flexible - When it comes to day trading, you are the sole person to determine the kind of markets you trade in and the types of stock you wish to trade. Each trading market has its advantages and disadvantages. Day trading allows you to scan the markets as a way of identifying the best depending on your risk profile, working hours, and trading plan. You can trade any time so long as the markets are open.

Lower commissions - Because you will be working with a broker, it is easy to get a broker that offers extremely low rates. This is a great plus for you if you intend to day trade on a long-term basis. With small commissions, you can easily pocket a good amount of profit since only a little percentage will go to the broker as interest rates.

Provides instant gratification - Day trading gives you the opportunity to make instant profits as soon as you start trading. Once you get onto the trading platform, you start selling or buying immediately.

Besides the numerous advantages of day trading, there are a few risks involved in the business that you also need to be aware of. They are as follows:

- *Information overload.* There is a wide variety of resources online today related to day trading. Most of this information is not accurate and can lead you to losing your capital. It is essential therefore, that you look for information from credible sources, and that you do not get too much of it as this may confuse you. For instance, some sites give traders the impression that day trading guarantees 100 percent profit, yet this is not true. If you come across such hype and you believe it, you may raise your expectations too high. This can cause you to invest your entire fortune in a deal you are not sure to win.

- *Time-consuming.* Day trading needs a lot of time since you must first study the market trends before placing your trades. It becomes difficult if you are doing the business alongside a regular job or other physical businesses. Your work schedule may hinder you from getting the best opportunities.

- May also need to trade outside regular working hours to be able to make a good profit from it. The trade becomes more complicated if you are following more than one market. You may end up overworking yourself, or overspending on a broker that is willing to carry out the trades on your behalf.

- *Too many risks involved.* Although day trading has a high potential for profit, it is too risky if you invest money that you are not willing to lose. It even becomes riskier if you engage in the trade using borrowed capital. Once you miss it, you are left with huge debts to settle.

- *Involves a lot of emotions.* When compared with other types of trading, day trading is more engaging in terms of emotions. Each time you make huge profits or losses, you may get too excited or too anxious, and this can lead to overtrading.

- *Requires accurate timing.* If you take too long to make decisions, then day trading may not work for you. The strategy requires that you make commitments too fast. To do this, you must have the right knowledge and tools for analyzing stock prices and market trends. You must also be confident of each move that you make since this must be done at adequate speeds for you to maximize on the available opportunities.

- *May get boring.* When the stock prices are highly volatile, you may be required to make quick decisions on which positions to buy or sell. However, once you have entered or closed positions, you will have nothing more to do except watch the market for more opportunities. The market may keep moving randomly for a long time as well without providing a chance for you to trade. This results in a waste of time on your part. You will need to monitor such a market to make a profit from it.

Day Trading Options

Most traders are aware of day trading stocks but have little information about using the same strategy for options. As you may know, options traders make money buying and selling puts and calls. Although options offer high leverage that looks more wonderful when used in day trading, day trading options is often associated with several challenges.

The number one challenge is that of the premium value, which seems to reduce the fluctuation of prices on a daily basis. The options market is also faced with a lot of liquidity challenges, thus reducing the amount of profit one can make from day trading. This means that if you choose options as your day trading instrument, you will need to deal with the following two issues:

- Loss of capital

- Price and market movement

Despite these downsides, it does make sense to apply day trading strategies on options. This is made more possible for traders with smaller accounts since the risk of losing capital remains minimal. One main reason that can make you interested in this kind of venture is the low costs involved. Options always require less money to trade. Instead of purchasing shares only to sell them the same day, you may consider buying options and selling them after a few hours at a profit, however small.

Another advantage that options offer for day traders is the ease with which they can enter and exit the market. When trading options, you can quickly get in and out of the market, then when trading bonds, stocks, and mutual funds. Options contract always give the trader a chance to opt out when the market is not too favorable. This means that you can use this strategy to minimize the risk of losing your capital significantly.

Just like stocks, you must be able to identify the right kind of options for day trading. One standard method used to do this is technical analysis. The technique enables you to predict stock price movements which in return assist you in determining whether or not to invest in a particular stock's options.

When day trading options, you must choose those options that feature less time value. These are options such as the near month in the money because they possess very little time value, thus offering you the best opportunity to make money. If you pick an option that has a high time value, you will make very little profit from it. The reason why low time valued options provide more profit potential is because most people often trade them. Their prices are also bound to change significantly within a single day. They also feature narrower bid-ask spreads.

Day trading options requires a lot of training and practice. If you try to figure out the business on your own, you may make regrettable mistakes along the way that can cost your entire capital. The more you practice, the more confident you will become. It is also essential that you get the right options trading systems that support day trading. A good system will reduce your responsibility of analyzing the market by giving you the necessary market data for your daily trading activities.

To avoid losing so much capital in options trading, you can engage the use of limit orders. The profit made from day trading options is often derived from the difference between the ask price and the bid price. This can be as low as 2% of the price of the option. One thing that makes options day trading more complicated is the pricing model. The cost of an option depends on several factors. This means that the price of an option can deflate or inflate more rapidly than other financial instruments. If you are not quick enough to identify and take advantage of these price movements, you may not realize any profits.

Chapter 5: Most Important Day Trading Strategies

The use of an effective management system for your money can begin to help you cultivate wins even if you only have 4 trades that are profitable out of the 10. So, take time to practice, then plan, and finally structure the threads that you do according to the management of your money and the allocation of your capital plan.

Consider the charges that the brokerage will be charging you. When day trading, you will see frequent transactions that will involve results of highly costly brokerage fees. Once you have done your research thoroughly, you will be able to plan the proper brokerage firm that you will go with through a carefully thought after plan. If you intend to only trade one or two per day, then you will need to find a broker that charges on a per trade basis plan. If you are planning to do day trading, then your volume is going to be high. In this instance, you should go with a staggered fee plan. The higher volumes that you have, the lower the cost will effectively be. You can also benefit from a plan that is a fixed rate. This will provide an unlimited amount of trades for one high fixed rate.

Trade Management and Position Sizing

Apart from all of this, the broker also offers services that include utilities for trading, and platforms that you can utilize for trading. The integrated solution for trading can be things such as combinations options, software trading, data for historical accuracy, tools that help with research, alerts for the trades, applications that chart with indicators that are technical along with features that are not already listed. Some of these features can be cost-effective or free, while some may come with a cost that could eat a hole in your profits or wallet. You should pick the features that are handy for your trading needs and avoid the ones that are subscribed to help with specific needs. A novice can start with basic low-cost brokerage fees that match the trading needs that are initially set and then later they can opt for modules and upgrades that are needed at this time.

You will also need to be able to simulate or reverse test the historical data of the strategies and trading charts. Once you have set a plan and it is ready, then you need to be able to simulate it to test the strategy and utilize the test to run a virtual test account with virtual money. Many of the brokers that you can hire will allow you to run a test for your account. You can also use the historical data to back test the strategy. This will give you an assessment that is realistic, as well as keep considerations for the cost of the brokerage and fees that subsequently will come up for the different various utilities.

Strategies

For most people, strategies are used in businesses to give business operations a sense of direction. However, most people ignore the fact that strategies are an important part of our everyday lives. They enable you to live your life in order and achieve even the simplest of goals. Basically, any journey undertaken without a strategy does not have an actual blueprint for addressing the various elements of the journey.

The significance of workable strategies cannot be underestimated when it comes to day trading. They form the framework under which the market can be studied, and traders leverage the most lucrative chances of making profits. In all day trading strategies, there is a need for in-depth technical analysis to establish the patterns of the price movements through charts and the different indicators for different strategies. The basic tenet of a day trading strategy is that emotions should be out of the strategy development process. Every strategy chosen should be based on facts, and there are various factors to be considered when choosing any strategy.

Trading Based on the Time of Day

Often, this fundamental analysis is going to be saved for long-term investing, something that you don't see much with day traders. It takes into account how the price of the company will go into the future when compared to where it is now, but these changes are often going to occur over weeks, months, or even years. Day trading takes place in one day. Because of this, most day traders will not use this information to help them make decisions about which stocks to trade in.

As a day trader, you probably won't spend a lot of time working on fundamental research. You could probably guess this by all the other strategies that we have in this book. Sure, most traders know that a demand in ethanol is going to make a difference in the price of corn during a particular time period. But day traders want to focus more on what the price is going to do right now compared to where it was a few minutes ago.

Chapter 6: Trading and Time

When one thinks of the different investment tools, if not the practice, of the investment in general, one cannot but considers the temporal factor. This is one of the factors that other miller discourages the trader. But why?

In these times, we are so used to the concept of *everything and immediately* we cannot wait any longer. We demand everything immediately, also losing track of time and the precious value of time.

Unfortunately, in online trading, you cannot expect to have everything and immediately, but above all, we cannot expect to become experienced traders and professionals in just under a month or worse than a week.

You cannot think of becoming an expert trader if you do not want to study and practice! In online trading, but also in investment, in general, it takes time to learn how to trade. Another advice that is not feasible at the moment is to think about spending some time to find a deserving, professional, and worthy investment and investment technique.

When trading, it must be done seriously and professionally. If, for example, we trade in a trading strategy based on currency trading, with a maximum payout of 65% for a positively closed trade, then we must enter the perspective that we must give money to work with a specific strategy.

If you are following the market trend, it will be counterproductive to exit the market because, in addition to losing its capital, you may not even get the desired return. That's why time is money, and it should not be wasted unnecessarily. Above all, hurry is a bad companion.

The time factor is also one of the main factors for which it is decided better to entrust its capital to a financial expert so that this is to make the choices for them. Very often, however, this trust is not always repaid by an increase in one's capital. Most often this capital is completely lost.

The Importance of the Right Time and Timing

Understanding when the right time to trade is very important. Giving money to mature is certainly one of the most determining factors for the success of your investment. The fundamental concept remains the same: within what you want to earn money and how to earn them.

To make sure that you know, in advance, how much you can earn and how to make money for us, you cannot rely on chance, and above all, we cannot expect to waste time but not even to demand everything immediately.

Everything has its time; also, in investment, they have their right times and their importance. As you can see, even the right timing serves to give way to the investment, to make your own cycle, and to express that reasonable expectation. The right setup also serves your capital to survive in any situation, resist negative moments, and always have the strength to start again.

Avoiding Risks

To better understand the risks involved in trading in risky strategies, it seems right to remember those that are the right principles. Suppose you can trade $10,000 in a strategy that is 50% risk. This strategy was put in place to double the capital within a maximum of 3. Highly risky strategy from our point of view as it could result in the total loss of the entire capital. This operation is recommended only to experienced traders.

With this example, we have made you understand how these operations allow you to double or triple the capital within a few months but also how you can lose all your capital in a matter of months. In fact, by implementing these dangerous strategies, you will also see the account halved, or entirely burned, within a few weeks.

To understand everything better, let's take another example. According to your trading strategies, you have traded on a particular asset with a strategy and think that this can give you a return of 50% within a month.

To not fall into error, we advise you to set the opposite goal or try to ask the question: how would it be if in half a month you lost half of the bill? Here is therefore explained and understood in a simple and fast way on what is the right time, but especially those that are the wrong strategies not to be adopted.

Limiting Damages of Social Trading

Many wonders if social trading is the right strategy to avoid wasting time and earning, thanks to social trading. Before proceeding, we remind you that social trading is not a risk-free form of trading, even if the risk, in this case, is reduced. To trade in social trading, we believe it is essential to operate for a period of time between 9 and 12 months minimum. This is for one simple reason. Before choosing an investment system, you must see the performance for at least a year. In this sense, there is no need to follow a trader, 24 hours a day, 365 days a year, but only that you have to consult all the data of all the operations performed during the year, perhaps with the help with special tools that simplify reading.

Once you understand how to trade, but above all, you understand how much trading and who you want to trade in, you have to consider the risk that you are willing to run. Beyond this limit, it is advisable to leave it alone.

In most cases, the conditions that have led you to make a certain investment choice must have solid foundations so that the investment can yield. That's why a period of 12 months is a period enough to make you understand if your investment is right or wrong.

Chapter 7:
What Should You Invest in to Be Profitable at Day Trading

Day trading is never the same for each day. A trader that has been trading for a length of time that is longer than a year will find that there is never two single days that are the same. Even though there are no similarities to the day, there are still patterns to the trends. They will occur over time, but they will be hidden within a random movement of price that takes place daily.

There are five-day setups that can occur over a specific amount of days, and at least one to two will occur within one day's time frame. However, they will not all occur in the same days' time period. Learning these trade setups will help you to exploit the potential of profit.

Context within the Patterns

Know the pattern and watching are not going to be enough for a successful day trading. These patterns will occur frequently; however, they only hold power when a specific context appears. Understand the action price in order to have a great entry in day trading. Identify when the traders are stuck, and the price will have cause to surge in a direction that is forced, meaning that the traders are selling. These setups will occur during emotional points. This is when traders will feel the pain or the greed. However, there is not going to be a definite that this will occur prior to big moves and it does not mean that there will be a result of big moves. We do not have an exact knowledge of what the traders think, or if the acts will take place based on these thoughts. By watching the action of the price patterns, you will see regular occurrences. These can produce results that are similar, which can improve the chance that the trade is profitable.

Impulse Buys Create Pullback That Results in a Consolidated Breakout

Trading can begin in a move that is strongly pulled in one single direction. This will take place within 5-15 minutes once the market opens for trading. The Stock Market calls this impulse wave. The price of the stock then will pull back and then stall out. This forms the consolidation so that the price will move sideways for about 3 minutes. It must occur within an impulse wave range. The pullback or consolidation has to occur lower than the price of open. Due to the initial impulse's direction, the investor will wait and experience the breakout that leaves the consolidation in the direction that is equal to the stock. Breakouts that head in the opposite direction are not traded. You want to consolidate and pull back if the price is rallied as soon as it opens. Next, you should wait for that price to be above the consolidated breakout price, and then the long trade is triggered. Consolidation must be, compared to others, small in relation to the impulse wave that is going to precede it. The pattern becomes less effective when the consolidation is compared to the large impulse wave. During the pullback, there should be a distinct pullback, as well as impulse waves that are distinct. If they are not distinct, then the effectiveness of the pattern is less and is avoided.

This pattern can be seen throughout the trading day and can be how a trend will form. This makes it a strategy that can be utilized on most frames of time and in the market. The most power-filled moves that a market will have will take place during the open of the day, which is why catching that first hour is important. It can mean important things for your portfolio and creates large impacts with your profitability. If it occurred later in the day, then it can create smaller moves in price.

Consolidation Reversal Breakout

Impulses are not always followed by pullbacks that are small. There can be big moves that head in one direction. However, they can grow in the movement to an even bigger direction that is opposite of the original one. This is a reversal in directionality. Focus on the big moves that are most recent.

If the price dropped to $0.20 at the open, then rallies at $0.30, do not get distracted with that first drop since it will not matter anyhow. You will now have what is called an impulse for the upside. Watch for the decline in price, just a bit, and then consolidate the stock. If the consolidation breaks $0.01 then stay longer. On the reverse, you can wait for the pullback to go to the opposite for the impulse. Then you will see the impulse has a smaller pullback.

Support/Resistance Reversal

This can be horizontal lines as well as diagonal lines. They will point you in a direction that the price has been reversed for at least 2 episodes prior. This will include that starting point. You should know that the support, as well as the resistance, is not a price exactly but an area. The setup is not required to take place near the support, nor the resistance. In other words, it can take place slightly below them or above them. This informs us to be on high alert, which is based on the fact that a reversal can be coming. Because of this, we will have to sit and wait for the consolidation that is near. There is a signal for trade if the break in price is above the support that is consolidation, or below consolidation that is resistant. If this signal occurs, the price of the trade that moved one cent higher than the consolidation close to the support and fall for resistance which occurs in the pattern. Leave the trade immediately if the resistance breaks above or below the support area. Consider that the trade of breakout could be applicable.

Breakout Area Is Strong

This is a fashionable way to trade a breakout that is either above or below the support major area. This is, however, one of the toughest. Although the strategies above are preferred, it is beneficial to explore strategic options for special situations that can arise. Look out for a level that has pushed back the price for multiple strategies that are basic. This price will rally and then will reach 25.25 however, and then it falls. Although it performs this dance several times, it can struggle to break through. Once the area has tested that price three times more, there can be an assured day trades that are noticed. Suddenly the price is reaching 25.26. This can signal shifts of importance. Breakouts do not guarantee moves that are big. You may fail to produce a move that is big, and the price can break boundaries that are strategic and sparing. By making moves away from the area, you should see a significant move away from the visual that is price tested. The pattern can lose the effectiveness that will significantly become rejected by the price that is near the area. This means that you should see several rejections that have happened over multiple times.

Once the traders push the level of the price back, it becomes a pattern of the power, despite the level that is sent. The price of the fact is opposite in direction for multiple occasions in the past. This shows that they have a greater resolve than the opposite directions the traders are going.

How Do You Make Day Trading Your Job?

If you have opened a broker account and begin to trade stocks, you are not required to have a license. If you plan to work for a firm to trade stocks, then you will need to acquire a series 7 license. This requires a specific number of hours in a classroom and then a test that will license you as a stockbroker. In order to sell and buy stocks for others, even as your own business, you will need the license. For your own personal financial gains, you can use an online brokerage account and earn money for yourself.

Series 7 Licensing is a test that is taken after you have completed a specific number of hours for training and learning. A job that involves trading stocks, bonds, and other securities and then you will need to follow the guidelines that are set up by the SEC. These regulations require you to have Financial Industry Regulatory Authority. This requirement states that you will need stock brokers and securities licensing representative. There are several options of FINRA registrations; however, the one that is most necessary will be the General Securities Registered Representative. This will require you to complete a class and pass the test that is called a series 7 exam. There are some limited exams that can provide you with limited securities capabilities. These allow you to trade specific bonds or options. Once you pass the proper test, you will complete the license requirements. This means that you can apply for your series 7 licenses.

In order to take the test and get licensed, you will need to have an employer sponsor you for the test. This means being sponsored by a FINRA member for the financial company service. You will need to be hired by a brokerage firm and then put through rigorous training and put you to work with a trading mentor. They will then sponsor you for the license as a securities trader. There are not that many pre-requisites that are required to be hired as a broker however, the licensing is required once you start to trade. Once you are hired you will have an agreement that states that you are employed only until and if you pass the series 7 test. The firm will oftentimes provide you with the training that is needed or the courses that will give you the ability to pass the test.

A self-employed trader is able to trade with no licensing requirements for trading within your own account with the broker. You have to use your own money and if you can not make it a successful career then you will lose your new career. If you begin with a smaller account and then use that to learn as you go, you will be able to profitably trade prior to turning this into your full-time work. Then you can trade the day job for a profession that is full-time and profitable.

Many of the day traders are trading stocks, although it is just as popular for a day trade to trade bonds, as well as currencies or even commodities. You generally need to look for securities that have these features:

- A trade volume that is large and highly liquid.

- Bonds that are volatile. You want changes that are frequent for the price because this allows the investor to make a quick profit.
- Stocks that are known by you. You need an understanding of what that particular stock's history in price is, and various events that designate how it will react to— economic shifts or earnings reports. This is a key deciding factor. Day traders will often only trade a selected few specific stocks, developing their expertise in the companies that they are trading. This will help them to narrow their focus so that they are not thinking too broad.
- Newsworthy stocks are a go to. News reports on a stock have a way of triggering investors to buy or sell them. As a day trader, you will need to be educated about these events so that you can make trades that are beneficial to you.

This day trade is done in one day. Although you already owned 10 ABC shares, you decided to open a position that is new in some more ABC shares with another purchase that are initial.

- Day Trade: (Buy 1 share of ABC, Sell 10 share of ABC)
- You start with 0 shares of ABC stock.
- Buy 1 share of ABC.
- Buy 2 shares of ABC.

- Buy 7 shares of ABC.
- Sell 1 share of ABC.
- Sell 5 share of ABC.
- Sell 4 share of ABC.
- Since there is one single change in only one direction within the buys and sells, this becomes a one-day trade.
- Day Trade: (Buy 1 share of ABC, buy 2 share of ABC, Buy 7 share of ABC, Sell 1 share of ABC)
- Two-day trades.
- Buy and Sell share of ABC 2x.
- You start out having 0 shares of stock in ABC.
- Buy 50 shares of ABC.
- Sell 15 share of ABC.
- Sell 35 share of ABC.
- Buy 10 shares of ABC.
- Sell 10 share of ABC.
- Since there are changes that are two x in the direction from buys to sell, this is now a trade for two-day.
- Day Trade 1: (Buy 50 share of ABC, Sell 15 share of ABC, Sell 35 share of ABC)
- Day Trade 2: (Buy 10 share of, Sell 10 share of ABC)

1. Trading with the same stock every time is a strategy that will help you succeed. Have one to three stocks that are you

skilled in and knowledgeable. Become the expert in those stocks and stick with what you know. Trade only these stocks and use strategies to calibrate the plan. You will have zero homework or research to do since you will always be trading the stocks that you already know more about that is necessary for trading. This will give you the advantage or the next day's trading since you will know what you are trading.

2. Pick the stocks that have volume enough for you to freely change your size of position depending on the bases on the volatility side. If your stock is one day volatile, then take size positions that are smaller than the trade and with stop losses that are slightly larger than the other as well as targets for the trade. If it is quiet for the stock, then you should increase your position so that you can compensate for the stop losses when they are smaller, and the targets are discussed later. This is a way for you to make an income that is decent regardless of how volatile it is within that particular day.

3. In day trading, the popular ETF happens to be S&P 500 SPDR (SPY). By day trading that ETF, or any other ETF/stock that you have chosen.

4. Run a screener for your stock every single week in order to find the two-four stocks which will provide a volume that is good and the exact volatility that you need, and then trade these stocks off and on all week. Do not trade any stocks that are not on your wish list or purchase any new stocks that you

have not fully researched. This can lead to losses due to uneducated guessing and poor strategy following. During the weekend, take some time to run your stocks or ETF screens again and again. This will help you find more stocks to add to your handful of stocks that you will be buying and selling throughout the week. You may notice that when you end up using the same stocks to trade week in and week out, for multiple weeks in a row, you are winning more each day, however having a strategy to switch up the ones you are buying will keep other day traders from catching onto your strategy and buying them out too early. If things are going super well, then you can stick with what you know and continue to trade the ones that you know and have done the research into. Many day traders are trading by sticking with what you have gained knowledge on and you are going to have success as a day trader. Over time you can develop strategies that work for not only these same stocks but others as well giving you an advantage over others who are only focusing on one set of stocks.

Chapter 8: From Mere Income Generation to Vocation

Look at day trading not as some desperate dash for cash. People who need cash yesterday should not even think about day trading, seriously. Close this book and look for a job. I can't emphasize that enough.

If you are in dire straits, you shouldn't be looking for quick cash online. You shouldn't look at day trading as a quick solution to all your financial problems. That's a recipe for financial disaster. If you think you're in a hole now, it's going to get worse. Let's face it, if you do things out of desperation, you will attract failure; that's just the way it works. You're not thinking clearly. You're focusing on what you're losing, and you often lose sight of the big picture.

You need to have the right mindset, and you have to understand that day trading is not just income generation. While it does a good job of providing solid income to a lot of people from all four corners of the globe, it's actually more than that. It's a vocation; it's a calling. I consider it an adventure because every single day is different from the day that came before.

Also, every single day, I'm given a tremendous opportunity, not to only learn about the psychology of the market, as evidenced in the up and down flow of the stocks I'm trading, I also learn about myself. I learn about my emotional states. I learn about my triggers, and all of this personal discovery is very exciting to me. I'm driven primarily by the thirst of learning something new.

You should adopt something similar. Focus on the adventure, focus on how you change and improve over time. Make no mistake about it, day trading is going to challenge you. It's going to challenge your level of self-discipline, your ability to control your impulses, and it also tests your goal-setting effectiveness. Instead of looking at these as hassles or problems that you need to overcome so you could reach a big payday, look at these as rewards in themselves.

Being more disciplined is a good thing. Being able to control your emotions is a tremendous asset. Learning how to set goals in such a way that you have a higher likelihood of becoming a reality is a great skill to have. Focus on these instead of the money. Now, I'm not saying that you should absolutely disregard the income generation aspect of day trading, but my point is that there are other important considerations to keep in mind. These are of equal if not greater importance.

Stay passionate

Again, you can't look at day trading with a desperate mindset. From my many years of experience living on this planet, I've learned that the more desperate I am to achieve some sort of result, the less likely that result will come to pass. Desperation seems to repel success.

What's the opposite of desperation? The answer is simple: passion. When you're passionate, you're curious. When you're passionate, you're in love with what you're doing; every little revelation excites you. It's not about your emotions per se; it's about your inner need to take things to the next level. Learn the patterns. Focus on your most successful moves. If you're able to do this in light of the discipline that you're building, you can convert "lucky trades" to predictable trades. This is the real mark of expertise.

Day traders who make a consistent income from day trading have gone past simply getting lucky to predictably producing results. Now, per trade, the results may not be all that impressive, but given the scale at which they trade, it's easy to see why they make tens of thousands, if not hundreds of thousands every single day. The good news is if they can do it, so can you.

Chapter 9: Momentum Trading

Momentum is at the heart of all-day trading as finding trades with the right amount of momentum is the only way you can reliably guarantee a profit on your trades. Luckily, it is not unrealistic to expect to find at least one underlying asset that is likely to move as much as 30 percent each day due to the fact that all underlying assets with this much momentum all tend to share a few common technical indicators.

Momentum stock anatomy

While it might seem difficult to understand how anyone could expect to pick a stock with the right momentum out of the thousands of possible choices, the fact of the matter is that all high momentum stocks typically have several things in common. In fact, if you were given a list of 5,000 stocks, using the factors below you could likely come up with a list of 10 or less.

Float: The first thing you are going to want to keep in mind is that the stocks with the highest momentum are generally going to have a float that is less than 100 million shares. Float refers to the total number of shares that are currently available and can be found by taking the total number of outstanding shares and subtracting out all those that are restricted or are, functionally speaking, no longer traded. Restricted shares are those that are currently in the midst of a lockup period or other, similar restriction. The less float a stock has, the more volatility it is going to contain. Stocks with smaller float tend to have low liquidity and a higher bid/ask spread.

Daily charts: The next thing you are going to want to look for is stocks that are consistently beating their moving average and trending away from either the support or resistance depending on if you following a positive or negative trend.

Relative volume: You are also going to want to ensure that the stocks you are considering have a high amount of relative volume, with the minimum being twice what the current average is. The average you should consider in this case would be the current volume compared to the historical average for the stock in question. The standard volume is going to reset every night at midnight which means this is a great indicator when it comes to stocks that are seeing a higher than average amount of action right now.

Catalyst: While not, strictly speaking, required, you may still find it helpful to look for stocks that are currently having their momentum boosted by external sources. This can include things like activist investors, FDA announcements, PR campaigns and earnings reports.

Exit indicators to watch

Besides knowing what a potentially profitable momentum trade looks like, you are also going to need to know what to look for to ensure that you can successfully get while the getting is good. Keep the following in mind and you will always be able to get out without having to sacrifice any of your hard earned profits.

Don't get greedy: It is important to set profit targets before you go into any trade, and then follow through on them when the trade turns in your favor. If you find yourself riding a stronger trend than you initially anticipated, the best choice is to instead sell off half of your holdings before setting a new and improved price target for the rest, allowing you to have your cake and eat it too.

Red candles: If you are not quite at your price target and you come across a candle that closes in the red then this is a strong indicator that you should take what you have and exit ASAP. If you have already sold off half of your holdings at this point, however, then you are going to want to go ahead and hold through the first red candle as long as it doesn't go so far as to actively trigger your stop loss.

Extension bar: An extension bar is a candle with a spike that causes dramatically increased profits. If this occurs you want to lock in your profits as quickly as possible as it is unlikely to last very long. This is your lucky day and it is important to capitalize on it.

Choosing a screener

Another important aspect of using a momentum strategy correctly is using a quality stock screen in order to find stocks that are trending towards the extreme ends of the market based on the criteria outlined above. A good screener is a virtually indispensable tool when it comes to narrowing down the field of potential options on any given day, the best of the best even let you generate your own unique filters that display a list of stocks that meet a variety of different criteria. What follows is a list of some of the most popular screeners on the market today. *StockFetchter.com:* StockFetcher.com is one of the more complicated screeners out there, but all that complexity comes with a degree of power that is difficult to beat. Its power comes from a virtually unlimited number of parameters that its users can add to filter, ensuring that you only see exactly the types of stocks you are looking for. It offers a free as well as a paid version, the free version allows you to see the top five stocks that match your parameters while the paid version, $8.95 per month, shows you unlimited results.

Finviz.com: This site offers a wide variety of different premade filters that are designed to return results on the most promising stocks for a given day. It is extremely user friendly as well and functions from three drop-down menus based on the type of indicator, technical, fundamental or descriptive, and lets you choose the criteria for each. The results can then be sorted in a myriad of different ways to make it as easy to find the types of stocks you are looking for as possible. The biggest downside to Finviz is that it uses delayed data which means it is going to be most effective for those who run evening screens so they are ready to go when the market opens.

Chartmill.com: This site allows users to filter stocks based on a number of predetermined criteria including things like price, performance, volume, technical indicators and candlestick patterns. It also offers up a number of more specialized indicators including things like squeeze plays, intensity, trend and pocket pivots. This site works based on a credit system, and every user is given 6,000 credits each month for free. Every scan costs a few hundred credits so you should be able to take advantage of a variety of their tools virtually free of charge. Additional credits then cost $10 per 10,000 or they have an unlimited option available for about $30 per month.

Stockrover.com: This tool is specifically designed to cater to the Canadian market in addition to the US stock market. It offers up a variety of fundamental filters in addition to technical and performance-based options. This tool also allows you to track stocks that are near their established lows and high, those that may be gaining momentum and even those that are seeing a lot of love from various hedge funds. Users also have the ability to create custom screens as well as unique equations for even more advanced screening. Users can also backtest their ideas to make sure that everything is working as intended. While their basic options are free to use, the more complex choices are gated behind a paywall that costs $250 for a year's subscription.

Know your filters

Day trading is about more than finding stocks that are high in volume, it is also about finding those that are currently experiencing a higher than average degree of movement as well. The following filters will help ensure that the stocks you find have plenty of both.

Steady volatility: In order to trade stocks that are extremely volatile with as little research as possible, the following criterion is a good place to start. While additional research is always going to be preferable in the long run, you can find success if you run this scan once a week and pay close attention to the results.

show stocks where the average day range (50) is above 5%

and the price is between $10 and $100

and average volume (30) is greater than 4000000

and exchange is not Amex

add column average volume (30)

add column average day range (50)

This list should ideally return stocks that have moved at least 5 percent every day for the past 50 days. It is important to use a minimum of 50 days, though 75 or 100 will produce even more reliable results overall. Results of this magnitude will show that the stock in question has moved a significant amount over the past few months which means it is likely to continue to do so for the near future. The second criterion will determine the amount you should be willing to pay per share and can be altered based on your personal preferences.

The third criterion will determine the level of volume that you find acceptable for the given timeframe. The example will look for volume that is greater than four million shares within the past month. From there, it will eliminate leverage ETFs from the results which can be eliminated if you are interested in trading ETFs. Finally, the add column will show the list of stocks with the largest amount of volume and the greatest overall amount of movement. Selecting these columns will then rank the results from least to greatest based on the criteria provided.

Monitor regularly: Alternately, you may want to do a daily search to determine the stocks that will experience the greatest range of movement in the coming hours. To do so, you will want to create a new list of stocks every evening to ensure that you will be ready to go when the market opens. This list can then be made up of stocks that have shown a higher volatility in the previous day either in terms of gains or in terms of losses. Adding in volume to these criteria will then help to make sure the results will likely continue to generate the kind of volume that day trading successfully requires. Useful filters for this search include an average volume that is greater than one million and the more you increase the minimum volume the fewer results you'll see.

When using this strategy, it is especially important to pick out any stocks that are likely to see major news releases before the next day as these are almost guaranteed to make the price move in a number of random directions before ultimately settling down. As such, it is often best to wait until after the details of the release are known and you can more accurately determine what the response is, though not so long that you miss out on the combination of high volume and high volatility. If you don't already have an earnings calendar bookmarked, the one available for free from Yahoo Finance! is well respected.

Monitor intraday volatility: Another option that is worth considering is doing your researching during the day as a means of determining which stocks are experiencing the greatest overall amount of movement at the moment. A vast majority of trading platforms provide this information in real time so it is easy to keep up to date on the changes that are happening at the moment. For example, if a stock opens at a point down 10 percent from its previous close and stays there you can then assume that there is no one biting on the action that the stock has available.

On the other hand, if the stock starts in a position where it is down 10 percent and then it just keeps dropping then that is a sign it is worth taking a closer look at. You may also find it useful to track stocks that are currently on their way to breaking through the established levels of resistance or support.

Look for bigger moves: In order to find the stocks that are likely to be making big moves sooner than later, without spending all of your free time doing research, you will want to primarily focus on the stocks that are showing a constant state of volatility. This is a great scan to run over the weekend in preparation for the coming week. On the other hand, you can run this scan every night to ensure you know what the differences are likely to be tomorrow. Furthermore, you may instead want to monitor volatility during the day as a means of determining which stocks have seen the most activity during the session in question.

Confirm the chart patterns

Once you have found a few stocks that your scanner indicates are likely to move in the direction you are hoping for, the next step is to double check this fact before you get your hopes up. To do so, you are going to want to review the relative candlestick charts and try and determine the correct entry point based on the point where the first pullback occurred. While many traders will simply buy in at the point where the pullback occurs, this then creates an additional volume spike which pushes the prices even higher. As such, finding the best entry point, in real time, is the key to long-term success.

Pennant: A pennant is a type of indicator that forms when there is significant movement in a given stock, followed by a sudden consolidation period that causes the pennant shape to form from a pair of converging lines. A breakout will then likely occur that goes in the same direction as the previous movement. This typically manifests as extreme movement first, followed by weaker volume from there as the tip of the pennant forms, followed then by more strong growth and even more post-breakout volume.

Cup and handle: The cup and handle pattern look like the bowl of a cup with the ride side handle. The pattern is u-shaped, charting a series of lows for the stock while the handle also slopes slightly downward. This is a sign that volume is going to remain low overall and that the stock in question should be avoided.

Triangles: Triangles are one of the most frequently seen patterns which tend to occur when the price range converges with the current high, during a period of naturally higher lows. When the convergence is at its peak the price action generates a triangle formation. You will find triangles that are symmetrical, descending and ascending but all three can be traded successfully in the same way. Triangles are going to remain viable trading indicators for differing amounts of time, but you can generally count on them to have two high points and two low swings. When the prices converge, they will then reach an apex and the closer in the timeline it is to this occurring, the tighter the price action ends up being and the closer the price is to experiencing a breakout.

Flags: Unlike triangles, flags can be thought of as a well-defined pause in an ongoing trend that occurs when the price finds itself confined to a small range between a pair of parallel lines. Flags generally only remain intact for a short period of time, lasting a handful of bars, at most. They also don't typically include dramatic price swings the way a common trading range or trend channel likely would. Flags can be either parallel or upward or downward sloping.

Rounded bottom: This pattern tracks a prolonged drop in price that will eventually rebound back to the point where it started. After the rebound occurs a reversal and breakout are likely to occur though it is best avoided as the new trend is likely not going to be strong enough to suit your day trading purposes.

Double top: This pattern is based on a pair of trendlines that are a fair distance apart from one another that track a price through a pair of significant downward movements before returning to the same high point when everything is said and done. After the price breaks through the support line you can expect significant downward movement coming up soon.

Head and shoulders: This indicator is created by three distinct price points, one that is higher than the other two which are on the same line. All three return to the same low point overall. A reverse head and shoulders are also possible where the outlier point is lower than the shoulder points rather than higher. When you see this indicator you can safely assume that a breakout is going to come at the support line to indicate the start of a new downward trend or upward trend in the case of a reverse head and shoulders.

Additional useful things to keep in mind

Be precise on your stops: In order to day trade successfully in the long-term, you need to keep a profit/loss ratio of a minimum of two to one. This means that you are often going to want to set a tight stop that is lower than the first pullback point of the stock that you are following. An ideal target is around 40 cents per share which means that you will want to set your stops 20 cents lower than your target. If you stop is greater than 20 cents you will want to manually end the trade and reassess. This is a useful strategy as it will allow you to generate stops at greater than 20 cents which means you will need to make $1 or more per unit on a trader which is far harder in many cases than you might expect.

You will also find that it is often easier to find success with 40 cents of profit as opposed to holding out for a $1 stop which means you need to make $2 of profit as the day trading market is simply too volatile for this to be useful in most cases. Your goal should then be to balance your overall level of risk across the entire timeframe you are trading in. The easiest way to determine the specific level of risk you are working with is to determine the distance between the entry point and the stop point. If you set a 20 cent stop and want to ensure your total risk amounts to less than $500 then you will still be able to deal in around 2,000 shares at a time.

Best time to trade: While you can successful trade using momentum at any point during the day, you are going to find the greatest degree of success, on average, between 9:30 am and 11:30 am. Even still, if there is an incoming news release then you are still going to want to hold off until you have a general idea of how the market is going to react. If you persist past 11:30 am then you will likely find the best results if you stick to the 5-minute chart exclusively. The 1-minute chart will become much too choppy after 11:30 am to ensure that your stops won't be trigger during normal price movement, making it very difficult to get anything to stick.

Analyze your results: Day trading successfully for any length of time means putting a heavy focus on the statistics behind what you are doing, specifically your overall win/loss ratio as only by monitoring this closely will you be able to regularly ensure that you are moving in the right direction. At the end of each week, your best bet is to determine your overall trading metrics. If you have a full month's worth of subpar metrics you will then want to reconsider your current strategy and see what you can do to improve things for the better overall.

Chapter 10: Deflation vs. Inflation How to Fight Them

Throughout this book and the other ones of our series, you've heard many things about inflation. It plays a crucial role in trading the currency market because central banks run their monetary policy based on the level of inflation.

Most central banks consider the two percent target to be healthy for steady economic growth, but that might change in the future. For now, it remains the line in the sand for central banking around the world.

Inflation refers to a rise in the price of goods and services. It stimulates consumption, and consumption is the one thing that makes an economy grow.

Here's an example. Assume you want to buy something, let's say a computer.

If the price of the computer rises, even a little, in a short period, you'll be tempted to buy it sooner out of fear of having to pay more for it in the future. In other words, you're not postponing the buying decision, and the item got sold.

The seller will place an order to the producer, the producer will start building supplies to manufacture it, people will have secure jobs, and the government has less unemployment benefits to pay. Not to mention people are happier because a growing economy brings high levels of personal satisfaction.

So that's the reason why inflation matters for central banking. When it rises over the two percent target, the central bank becomes alarmed. There's too much money in the economy, and the bank will start a "draining" process, by raising the interest rates.

By doing that, it stimulates commercial banks to stop lending to businesses and the general population, and simply put their excess reserves in overnight deposits with the central bank. For that, they'll receive guaranteed interest, without taking the unnecessary risks associated with lending.

The example with the computer used here shows why a certain inflation level helps an economy. But what do you do when the price of a good or service falls?

Clearly, the first reaction of most human beings is that it's now a bargain and that's great for a deal. It may be so, but that's only on first look, and it's a circumstance you don't want to have for an extended period of time.

If prices keep falling, people will keep postponing their purchasing decisions – out of fear of missing out on an even lower price in the future. Retailers won't sell anymore, inventories will rise, producers will have to lay off people, unemployment will rise, and the economy will fall into recession.

When inflation falls below zero, it is said that the economy reached deflationary territory, and that's very difficult for central banks to fight. One clear response is to cut interest rates, but up until recently, central banks never dropped the rate below zero.

Nowadays, however, negative rates are a reality, and some economies remain resilient despite such stimulus. We can say, without a shadow of doubt, that between inflation or deflation, the second one is far worse for an economy and population than the first one is.

So, from this moment on, when you see the prices of goods and services dropping, think twice whether it's a good or a bad thing. Not only because it doesn't bring anything good for the economy, but it signals deeper and larger problems ahead.

Chapter 11: Portfolio Diversification

Day traders generally execute trades in the course of a single trading day while investors buy and hold stocks for days, weeks, months, and sometimes even a couple of years. In between these two extremes are other forms of trading. These include swing trading and position trading, among others. I strongly suggest readers take seriously the option of diversifying his trading account and other than day trading options strategies, add a mid or long term approach in order to get fewer fluctuations in the overall portfolio. That's why you will learn here the basics of the portfolio diversification because if you are a complete beginner, using only day trading strategies, will expose you to huge loss over a long period of time, due to large intrinsic leverage of options and day trading strategy in general. Swing trading is where a trader buys an interest in a commodity or stock and holds the position for a couple of days before disposing of it. Position trading, on the other hand, is where a trader buys a stake in a commodity or stock for a number of weeks or even several months. While all these trades carry a certain element of risk, day trading carries the biggest risk.

A trader with the necessary skills and access to all the important resources is bound to succeed and will encounter a steep learning curve. Professional day traders work full time, whether working for themselves or for large institutions. They often set a schedule which they always adhere to. It is never wise to be a part-time day trader, a hobby trader, or a gambler. To succeed, you have to trade on a full-time basis and be as disciplined as possible.

Introduction to Diversification

Diversification is considered an effective risk management technique. It is widely used by both traders and investors. The gist behind this approach is that investing funds in just single security is extremely risky as the entire trade could potentially go up in smoke or incur significant losses.

An ideal portfolio of securities is expected to fetch a much higher return compared to a no-diversified portfolio. This is true even when compared to the returns of lower-risk investments like bonds. Generally, diversification is advisable not only because it yields better returns but also because it offers protection against losses.

Diversification Basics

Traders and investors put their funds in securities at the securities markets. One of the dangers of investing in the markets is that traders are likely to hold onto only one or two stocks at a time. This is risky because if a trade was to fail, then the trader could experience a catastrophe. However, with diversification, the risk is spread out so that regardless of what happens to some stocks, the trader still stands to be profitable.

At the core of diversification is the challenge posed by unsystematic risks. When some stocks or investments perform better than others, these risks are neutralized. Therefore, for a perfectly balanced portfolio, a trader should ensure that they only deal with assets that are non-correlated. This means that the assets respond in opposite ways or differently to market forces.

The ideal portfolio should contain between 25 and 30 different securities. This is the perfect way of ensuring that the risk levels are drastically reduced and the only expected outcomes are profitability.

In summary, diversification is a popular strategy that is used by both traders and investors. It makes use of a wide variety of securities in order to improve yield and mitigate against inherent and potential risks.

It is advisable to invest or trade in a variety of assets and not all from one class. For instance, a properly diversified portfolio should include assets such as currencies, options, stocks, bonds, and so on. This approach will increase the chances of profitability and minimize risks and exposure. Diversification is even better if assets are acquired across geographical regions as well.

Best Diversification Approach

Diversification focuses on asset allocation. It consists of a plan that endeavors to allocate funds or assets appropriately across a variety of investments. When an investor diversifies his or her portfolio, then there is some level of risk that has to be accepted. However, it is also advisable to devise an exit strategy so that the investor is able to let go of the asset and recoup their funds. This becomes necessary when a specific asset class is not yielding any worthwhile returns compared to others.

If an investor is able to create an aptly diversified portfolio, their investment will be adequately covered. An adequately diversified portfolio also allows room for growth. Appropriate asset allocation is highly recommended as it allows investors a chance to leverage risk and manage any possible portfolio volatility because different assets have varying reactions to adverse market conditions.

Investor opinions on diversifications

Different investors have varying opinions regarding the type of investment scenarios they consider being ideal. Numerous investors believe that a properly diversified portfolio will likely bring in a double-digit return despite prevailing market conditions. They also agree that in the worst-case situation will be simply a general decrease in the value of the different assets. Yet with all this information out there, very few investors are actually able to achieve portfolio diversification.

So why are investors unable to simply diversify their portfolios appropriately? The answers are varied and diverse. The challenges encountered by investors in diversification include weighting imbalance, hidden correlation, underlying devaluation, and false returns, among others. While these challenges sound rather technical, they can easily be solved. The solution is also rather simple. By hacking these challenges, an investor will then be able to benefit from an aptly diversified platform.

The Process of Asset Class Allocation

There are different ways of allocating investments to assets. According to studies, most investors, including professional investors, portfolio managers, and seasoned traders actually rarely beat the indexes within their preferred asset class. It is also important to note that there is a visible correlation between the performance of an underlying asset class and the returns that an investor receives. In general, professional investors tend to perform more or less the same as an index within the same class asset.

Investment returns from a diversified portfolio can generally be expected to closely imitate the related asset class. Therefore, asset class choice is considered an extremely crucial aspect of an investment. In fact, it is the single more crucial aspect for the success of a particular asset class. Other factors, such as individual asset selection and market timing, only contribute about 6% of the variance in investment outcomes.

Wide Diversifications between Various Asset Classes

Diversification to numerous investors simply implies spreading their funds through a wide variety of stocks in different sectors such as health care, financial, energy, as well as medium caps, small, and large-cap companies. This is the opinion of your average investor. However, a closer look at this approach reveals that investors are simply putting their money in different sectors of stocks class. These asset classes can very easily fall and rise when the markets do.

A reliably diversified portfolio is one where the investor or even the manager is watchful and alert because of the hidden correlation that exists between different asset classes. This correlation can easily change with time, and there are several reasons for this. One reason is international markets. Many investors often choose to diversify their portfolios with international stocks.

However, there is also a noticeable correlation across the different global financial markets. This correlation is clearly visible not just across European markets but also in emerging markets from around the world. There is also a clear correlation between equities and fixed income markets, which are generally the hallmarks of diversification.

This correlation is actually a challenge and is probably a result of the relationship between structured financing and investment banking. Another factor that contributes to this correlation is the rapid growth and popularity of hedge funds. Take the case where a large international organization such as a hedge fund suffers losses in a particular asset class.

Should this happen, then the firm may have to dispose of some assets across the different asset classes. This will have a multiplier effect as numerous other investments, and other investors will, therefore, be affected even though they had diversified their portfolios appropriately. This is a challenge that affects numerous investors who are probably unaware of its existence. They are also probably unaware of how it should be rectified or avoided.

Realignment of Asset Classes

One of the best approaches to solving the correlation challenge is to focus on class realignment. Basically, asset allocation should not be considered as a static process. Asset class imbalance is a phenomenon that occurs when the securities markets develop, and different asset classes exhibit varied performance.

After a while, investors should assess their investments then diversify out of underperforming assets and instead shift this investment to other asset classes that are performing well and are profitable in the long term. Even then, it is advisable to be vigilant so that no one single asset class is over-weighted as other standard risks are still inherent. Also, a prolonged bullish market can result in overweighting one of the different asset classes which could be ready for a correction. There are a couple of approaches that an investor can focus on, and these are discussed below.

Diversification and the Relative Value

Investors sometimes find asset returns to be misleading, including veteran investors. As such, it is advisable to interpret asset returns in relation to the specific asset class performance. The interpretation should also take into consideration the risks that this asset class is exposed to and even the underlying currency.

When diversifying investments, it is important to think about diversifying into asset classes that come with different risk profiles. These should also be held in a variety of currencies. You should not expect to enjoy the same outcomes when investing in government bonds and technology stocks. However, it is recommended to endeavor to understand how each suits the larger investment objective.

Using such an approach, it will be possible to benefit more from a small gain from an asset within a market where the currency is increasing in value. This is as compared to a large gain from an asset within a market where the currency is in decline. As such, huge gains can translate into losses when the gains are reverted back to the stronger currency. This is the reason why it is advisable to ensure that proper research and evaluation of different asset classes are conducted.

Currencies should be considered

Currency considerations are crucial when selecting asset classes to diversify in. take the Swiss franc for instance. It is one of the world's most stable currencies and has been that way since the 1940s. Because of this reason, this particular currency can be safely and reliably used to measure the performance of other currencies.

However, private investors sometimes take too long choosing and trading stocks. Such activities are both overwhelming and time-consuming. This is why, in such instances, it is advisable to approach this differently and focus more on the asset class. With this kind of approach, it is possible to be even more profitable. Proper asset allocation is crucial to successful investing. It enables investors to mitigate any investment risks as well as portfolio volatility. The reason is that different asset classes have different reactions to all the different market conditions.

Constructing a well-thought-out and aptly diversified portfolio, it is possible to have a stable and profitable portfolio that even outperforms the index of assets. Investors also have the opportunity to leverage against any potential risks because of different reactions by the different market conditions.

An Example

An investor has a total of $100,000 to invest. The best approach is to put the funds in a diversified portfolio, but the challenge is properly or adequately balancing the portfolio. The first step is to check out market conditions and then conduct an assessment of possible returns versus any likely risks. As such, the investor can choose to invest in very secure investments that are likely to produce long-term income.

Such an investment can include between 10 and 12 stocks that are highly diversified. These are generally stocks from different sectors, industries, and countries. This kind of diversification helps to leverage against any possible risks and also ensures the portfolio is thoroughly mixed.

Portfolio Diversification Approach

Disciplined Investing is a Must.

Everyone is in agreement that diversification is basically the right approach. However, as an investor, there is a need to be disciplined even as you invest and diversify your investments. Investing is an art form. Put your money in equities but not all your money. Instead, think of yourself as a mutual fund manager then come up with a list of companies to invest in. You can also invest in funds and trusts like REITs or real estate investment trusts and exchange-traded funds. It is also advisable to go beyond local borders and invest globally. This way, you spread your risk around and stand chances of enjoying much better returns.

Consider Investing in Bonds and Index Funds

Apart from investing in stocks across numerous sectors, a trader may also want to invest your funds in certain fixed-income or index funds. When you invest in securities that closely keep an eye on a major index is highly recommended as you will be able to monitor progress and known when to make adjustments and so on. Such funds charge very low fees, and you will be able to easily track your investments.

Portfolio Building is a Continuous Process

Try to always grow your investments. If you receive some cash from somewhere, you can consider investing part of the entire amount into your investment portfolio. Also, keep adding regular amounts to your portfolio. You can, for instance, add about $500 each month to this portfolio to grow it at a much faster pace.

Learn the Best Exit Times

Sometimes we tend to get comfortable with the purchase-and-hold approach. This is true, especially when our investments are on autopilot. Yet a smart investor you need to keep looking out for events and special moments. Always remain abreast of events and be ready to act depending on the nature of the event. This way, you will be prepared for the moment when you have to cut your losses and exit your trades.

Watch Out for Commissions

As a trader, you need to remember that there are commissions to be paid as well as fees and charges. These charges can add up over time and become a significant amount. Therefore, keep a lookout for the charges and ensure that they are always maintained at manageable levels. In general, investing should be informative, fun, rewarding, and educational.

However, you need to be disciplined as a trader in order to be profitable in the long term and possibly outperform some of the major indices. Apart from the buy-and-hold strategy, you should diversify your portfolio, keep growing your portfolio, and learn to read the signs and know when the time is right to exit a trade. This way, your trading ventures will become extremely fruitful in the long run.

Diversification Summary

Diversification can easily be summed up using a single phrase. Never put all your eggs in one basket. This is as simple as it gets. However, the statement does not explain exactly how to go about diversification.

The idea behind portfolio diversification is simple. A trader needs to diversify into a whole group of securities, and these should be from different asset classes. It would be wrong for a portfolio to contain only stocks from one company only. Should anything happen to that company, then the investor or even trader stands to suffer huge losses, and such losses can end the investment or trade dreams of a trader.

When an investment is split into two or more different companies and asset classes, then the potential risk facing a certain product is drastically reduced. Apart from investing in more than one company, it is also a great idea to put funds in other securities such as bonds, futures, and currencies.

Traders need to develop an asset allocation strategy. Such a strategy should mostly focus on investment in stocks and bonds. Asset allocation is closely related to diversification because when done properly, asset allocation leads to a sustainably diversified portfolio.

There are other additions that can secure a portfolio and improve its diversification. These include mutual funds that consist of varied securities. A mutual fund is generally a diversified investment so diversifying into a fund helps in further diversification of a portfolio.

It is advisable to learn how to arrive at a desirable risk to reward ratio. Such a ratio can help determine the best way to diversify funds. A risk-reward ratio provides the opportunity to enjoy a particular rate of return for those willing to assume a small level of risk. Therefore, those willing to take on higher risk levels are more likely to benefit more compared to those assuming lower levels of risk.

There are some who prefer lower risk levels because perhaps of their limited resources or perhaps they prefer minimal complications. Such investors simply mirror a single and balanced fund. Others choose to simply invest in the fund. However, this can be viewed as simplistic by others who may wish for a more diversified approach.

In conclusion, diversification is key for sustainable investment, especially in the long run. It is not just more profitable but provides a risk management element into the entire investment portfolio process. Finding a suitable balance in the choice of assets provides a great approach to apt diversification.

Reducing Day Trading Risks

Risk Management.

With any trade, risk management is an essential component despite the fact that it is often overlooked. It is crucial that day; traders learn about risk management if they are to successfully trade and remain profitable in the long term. The good news is that there are some simple strategies that can be adopted to ensure that trades are protected and risk management appropriately.

Basically, risk management is one of the most important aspects of the life of any serious day trader. The reason is that a trader can actually see 90% of their trades make money, but the 10% losing money may result in a net loss if there is no proper risk management. Therefore, it is important to plan all trades carefully and to take measures to protect all trades against any losses.

Trades should be Planned Appropriately

It is a well-known fact that a good strategy will win the war rather than the battle. A good day trader needs to plan and come up with a winning strategy as the first step. A lot of traders often live by the mantra, "Plan the trade and trade the plan." This is also very similar to war planning because those who plan properly are likely to win.

Chapter 12: Money Management

What is Money Management?

Money management is not a new aspect of the financial management world. It started when there was a rise of capitalism. When the economy was under a system that was dominated by private owners, they had their private properties and gained on the profits. Money Management started in around 1600, and individuals only survive by depending on how effectively they get their income. In the present age, to be successful financially involves having the ability and the zeal to save more, and lean on investing any surplus.

Money management is a term to refer to the many ways people manage their financial resources. It ranges from budget planning in regards to their income. Money management involves planning and purchasing items that are important to you. Without planning well and lack of money management skills, the amount a person has will always not be enough for them.

Before anyone starts on the money management journey, you need to be aware of the assets and liabilities that you have. Some of the examples of Personal assets and properties are cars, home, retirement, investment, and bank accounts. On the other hand, personal liabilities are loans, debts, and mortgages. To be able to know your net worth, you should see the difference between your assets and liabilities. When the liabilities are higher than the assets, then you have a lower net worth. Having excellent money management skills, you will be able to avoid this.

Goal setting helps in Money management. Without goal setting, you will be worried about daily bill management; this can adversely affect your long term goals. With goal setting, you can have a clear view of the expenses needed to, and which needs to be cut out. A perfect example is when you have a goal of getting a car worth $30,000, your goals will be to cut down your expenses. Similar to someone whose goals are to get a $20,000 car?

After planning and knowing your goals, start creating your budget. A budget is an estimation of income for a defined period of time — a tool which will assist you in managing your money well. With a budget, you will be able to save some cash and be able to minimize impulse buying. An example of a reasonable budget will be to allocate $250 for entertainment and miscellaneous expenses a month after settling the basic needs. If your income increases, it would be advisable to add the extra income to your savings plan and not adding it to the expenses budget.

When budgeting, you will have multiple accounts to manage. For example, you may have an emergency fund and saving accounts. By doing this, you will avoid the temptations of spending the funds on impulse buying. The retirement plan should be kept separate from the other accounts. There are different software that you can use to assist you in money management. An example of a money management software is Quicken; it helps in tracking your various accounts and ensuring your saving and spending goals are on the right track.

The different aspects of money management include analyzing, planning, and executing a financial portfolio. The financial portfolio includes investment types, taxes, savings, and banking. In business management, there are economic variables that might affect your business finances. The best Money Management skills are to be able to access and control all the factors that might affect your financial position.

You can achieve your set goals through excellent money management. A dream of owning a home without using student loans, and be able to have a stress-free life from debts. Have a better plan to be able to deal with unpredictable events that can affect your finances; like loss of employment, serious illness. With Money Management, you will be able to have some savings that will cover your unexpected events.

Internet is a global computer network that contains information and provides communication. Banking, investment, and insurance needs did not exist before. In the past days, customers had restrictions on decisions making in their financial matters, with less information on their options in their local areas. With the lack of internet connection, there was limitation and restrictions on where to find the right information. People had to go shopping for different items, like furniture and electronics. And also the purchasing of mortgages and insurance policies.

Money Management Skills

Do you know your income expenditure? Do you know your shopping, clothing and entertainment expenses?

Money Management is a life skill which is not in the school curriculum. Most people learn it from our parents on how to handle money. Since most people didn't learn about financial skills in school, you can still learn them now. Here are some of the Money management skills that you can follow to improve your skills.

Set a Budget

Track how you spend your money. Do you spend on food, movies, entertainment, and clothes? Do you frequently have an overdraw of your bank account? If this is true, then set a budget. Check your bank statements and note down how much is your expenditure categorically. You will find out how much wastage of money you are not aware of.

Spend wisely

Have a shopping list when you go to the grocery store? Do you first check the price of an item before putting the item in your basket? Use coupons if available. Use online resources and mobile apps to stay focused on your expenditure.

Monitor your spending! By not being attentive to these small tips, you will keep on losing money. It takes time to get coupons, and It takes some effort to find coupons and writing a shopping list and checking the price of an item before buying, it will all be worth it in the long run.

Balance your books

Most people rely on going online to look at their bank balance. By doing this, you won't be able to know how much you are spending at the moment. The best advice is to be accountable by recording all your expenses; you will have avoided overspending.

Set a plan

You must have a plan for you to accomplish anything. For you to go from location A to B, it won't be possible without a GPS to show the routes. You will end up driving aimlessly going nowhere.

This is similar to not having a financial plan. You will always be broke and not knowing where your money is spent on. "Where did that money go?" With a great plan, you will be able to track your money and expenditure.

Think like an investor

The education system does not teach about handling money, mainly how to invest in growing your wealth. The rich people did not just save $500 a month; they learned how to grow their savings and invest. Turning that $500 into $1000, then into $10,000 and eventually into $100,000 and more.

By investing and growing your money, you will have secured a stable financial future. Think like an investor, and see your money grow.

Have the same financial goals with your partner/spouse

If you're married and you have a joint bank account, then learn to work together. You must both agree with the financial goals. Make a budget and also see a financial adviser to learn how to invest your money. You must ensure that you have the same financial goals and stay focused.

Save Money

Have a strong commitment to saving your money and securing your future. You can improve your financial situation and make it better! But you need to start with the decision to do so. Make a decision to start saving your money and improving your management skills.

Importance of Money Management

Sticking to a budget and living within your means – is proper money management. Look for great price bargains and avoiding bad deals when purchasing. When you start earning more money, understanding how to invest will become an essential way of reaching your goals like having down payment for a home. Understanding the importance of excellent money management will help you achieve your plans and future goals. Some of the importance of Money Management are:

Better Financial Security

Being cautious of your expenditures and saving, you will be able to save enough for the future. Saving will give you financial security to deal with any unexpected expenses or emergencies like loss of employment, your car breaking down or even saving for a holiday. Having savings, you will not have to use a Credit card to settle crises. Saving is a crucial part of money employment as it helps you build your financial security for a secured future.

Take Advantage of Opportunities

You may encounter opportunities to invest in a business to make more money or an exciting experience like a good deal on a holiday vacation. A friend may inform you of a great investment opportunity or get a great once-in-a-lifetime dream holiday vacation. It can be frustrating not having the money to jump right to these opportunities.

Pay Lower Interest Rates

With excellent money management skills, you can determine your credit score. The highest score means you pay your bills on time and with low-level total debt. Having a higher credit score, you can save more of what you have and have a lower interest rate for car loans, mortgages, credit cards, and even car insurance. And there is the chance to brag to your friends about your high credit score at the parties.

Reduce Stress and Conflict

Paying your bills on time can have a relieving feeling. But on the other hand, being late in paying your bills cause stress and have a negative impact like shutdown in your gas and water supply. Always being broke before your next paycheck can bring conflict and, a significant amount of stress for, couple. And, as we all know, stress brings health problems, experts say, like hypertension, insomnia, and migraines. Being aware of how you can manage your finances, so you have extra cash and savings can put your mind at ease. You will enjoy a stress-free life.

Earn More Money

With your income growing, your financial planning will not only include budgeting for monthly expenses but also figuring out where to invest the extra cash that has accumulated. Knowing different kinds of investments for example stocks and mutual funds, you can earn more money from the investments than what you could have made by leaving the money in your savings account in your bank. But be aware not all investments are recognized as a good investment idea, for example, offshore casinos. One of the best benefits of having investments, you can be at work earning monthly income, and your investments, on the other hand, are making more money for you.

More saving and time

Excellent money management can assist in avoiding your finances from spiraling out of control. It is easy to be in debt if you are unaware of how all your income it's spent monthly. Effective money management means better use of your spare time. You can spend time with your family and friends, by having a clear budget, you will be able to plan for fun days out as you will have available cash to do so.

Peace of mind

Excellent money management gives you some level of calm and peace of mind. With your income and the savings, you can handle any financial demands with the confidence that you have the resources to handle any need that will arise.

Best Money Managers

When developing your investment strategy, you will find yourself seeking some assistance. A well-chosen money manager can help you achieve your financial goals. Research is vital, find the right money manager who will be the perfect fit for your financial goals. There is a lot of information you can get to be able to find a money manager. You can rely on referrals, the internet, or financial companies to get the right money manager for you. In this segment we will go through what a money manager is. How does it work? What is the difference between a money manager and a financial advisor? What is the role of a money manager? What are the pros and cons of having a money manager? And what are the fees required?

Who is a Money Manager?

A money manager, also known as investment managers or portfolio managers. It's an individual or a firm which manages investments portfolio and provide personalized financial advice to an individual or institutional investor. Money managers offer advice to clients about the steps they should take to increase their returns.

How does it work?

Money managers earn a fee for their services and not a commission. In some cases, a client will pay a percentage of the managed assets to their money manager. In this way, both the client and the money manager will work hard towards the success of the portfolio. Here is an example illustrating how money managers work:

Suppose Mary has $20,000 and she wants to invest the money. She will find a money manager to manage her new portfolio. Then she schedules a meeting with the money manager. The money manager inquires about Mary's investment goals, the risk if the investment is a short-term or long-term, etc. Based on Mary's feedback, the money manager will choose a set of securities that will help Mary achieve her financial goals. The money manager will monitor Mary's portfolio on a monthly fee basis, the performance and the value of the portfolio.

What's the difference between a money manager and a financial advisor?

When it comes to your finances, doing it alone can be intimidating as you try to understand the game plan. You need to find the right professional to assist you in meeting your goals.

A financial advisor and a money manager have a lot in common, the two jobs are different, and they can't be handled by one person. A financial advisor is also known as wealth managers. A financial advisor understands the specifics of the client's economic life and creates a detailed investment plan, that is is also known to help the client meet their financial goals. A money manager focuses on managing the strategy your portfolio is invested in.

The role of a money manager:

A good money manager focuses on successfully managing your portfolio strategies, and should be able to meet the following expectations:

√ To consistently manage investments portfolio with their stated investment objectives

√ Appropriate risk management

√ Avoid unnecessary turnover within the management team

√ Operate transparently

What are the pros and cons of having a money manager?

When you have a financial goal, you want it to be a success. One of the ways to achieve that is by getting an expert to help you achieve your goals. Do you have some savings which you are thinking of investing? Then you need a money manager for you to achieve your goals of investing. You need a trustworthy and focused money manager. Consider a lot of things before hiring one. To be able to make the right choice, here are some of the pro and cons of having a money manager:

The pros:

Your money manager knows the financial environment

Your money manager can assist you in constructing an income statement and help you understand the market competition. With a great money manager, you can get an excellent customized financial plan and gain essential insights that will help you in your journey.

Your financial manager will make sure your money financial wisely

If there ever a time that you needed to make sure that your cash made the most significant impact, it's now. With a strained economy, there is no room for errors. Your money manager will assist you to avoid the risks and make sure your money it's spent in a way that will bring the best returns. Wondering whether to expand? If you are also thinking of increasing your investment, a money manager makes the smartest and best-informed decisions and assist you with any questions that you might have.

A money manager will free up your time to do what's most important

Your money manager will take away the stress of financial oversight, and this allows you to focus on other vital parts of life.

Your money manager can help your business function well

If you run a business, the money manager can help you with your business. To find out why invoices taking too long without getting paid, why your business is losing cash, and you are not sure where the wastage is happening. The money manager can implement control measures that allow you to easily track your money movement.

The cons:

Your money manager could be expensive

The main reason for not hiring a money manager is the cost! Your concern is a valid one. Money managers are highly qualified and experienced and usually request higher charges. Who can afford an expensive money manager when you have come a long way without him or her up to this point? The solution here is to do your research to get an affordable money manager who will give you the best quality results as well.

Performance Not Guaranteed

Although your money is managed professionally by the money manager, there are still no guarantees. In a bad market day, even the best money manager may lose money.

Lack of Control

You might not have the time or the knowledge to wisely invest your money; it will not be 100% comforting to some people to hand over control of their money to a stranger.

What is a Money Management Rule?

Investing doesn't necessarily need you to be an expert in the field. As a matter of fact, you don't need to be rich to begin investing. However, most people fail to manage their money because they don't know where to start. Here are some of the rules of money management to guide you through your journey:

Have a plan

How much are you planning to invest? When do you want to invest? When do you plan to exit? You can start from the end and determine how much money you need to invest. Plan for the future, towards financial freedom.

Time is money

The earlier you start investing, the better advantage you will have. Time is the biggest asset you have. For every time you invest include retirement savings too. There isn't anything that can make up for the effect of compound interest. If you end up losing money in the market, there is enough time for you to recover when you need it. For example, if you invest $1k for five years, you can make equal to $1.8k or $2k in 6 years, assuming the rate of return is the same. It amounts to a 10% difference if you invest one year later.

Do you sincerely think the 10% difference is worth falling off your investment? Never use the "it's too early to start investing" phrase as an excuse to keep your money under the mattress. It's much better to begin late than never.

It's emotional

We usually make most of our money decisions emotionally like greed, nervousness, and fear. To be able to focus on your long-term investment plan, do not check your account on a daily basis. There are regular fluctuations in the market and individual stocks. If to are making long-term investments, you don't need the stress of constant checking.

A lot of investors get fear after checking the media, and they end up buying or selling their investments at the wrong time. To avoid making such a mistake, be ready, and try to stay calm.

Financial Goals

Set short term and long term financial goals. Grow your goals and adjust them monthly. Correct your failures and enjoy the success.

Save Money

Saving for regular expenses like home maintenance and car expenses. It's advisable to save 5-10 percent of the net income. Save 3 to 6 months of your income to an emergency fund.

Financial Status

Set different expenses and include your debt payments too. Compare the amount of money coming in and what's going out. Know your debts and net income.

Set a Budget

Budget and closely monitor your spending plan.

Record Expenditure

Carefully monitor your money. You can note down and adjust appropriately.

Know the Difference Between Needs and Wants

To quickly know the difference, a need is something that is required for survival. For example, food, shelter, clothes, and water while a want is everything else. Wants to make life a little bit enjoyable. Put more fused on Needs first. And spend on the Wants only after you have taken care of your needs.

Use Credit Sensibly

Consider credit for planned purchases only. Take the amount that you can comfortably afford to purchase on credit. Credit payments shouldn't exceed 20% of net pay. Don't borrow from a creditor to settle debt to another creditor.

Settle your bills on time

Keep a higher credit score. Talk to your creditors in advance to explain your situation, if you won't be paying your bills on time.

Tips Used for Money Management

Money management is a delicate topic. For most individuals, it can be overwhelming and intimidating. You may have retirement savings, or not having enough emergency savings. Whatever your concern is, having a good handle of your finances is the best option. Here are some money management tips to get you started.

Manage Monthly Pay

Know your monthly income to better manage your money. Monthly budget, including rent or mortgage payments, gas bills, and other expenses like student loan payments, can be stressful to keep track of. However, making small changes can help you reduce your debts and expenses. Add extra into your monthly payments. Another advice is to increase payments over a year, or another option is to sign up for an automatic payment program. This will assist you to save time and money every month, as payments are deducted automatically from your savings account.

Track Your Spending Habits

Play detective with your finances. You will need to check the financial status by yourself. It might be overwhelming by limiting yourself to monthly expenses. Check out credit card statements, utilities bank account statements and also electronic payment records. Create a spreadsheet or use a pen and paper and track your expenses.

You can also categories your expenses. For example, labeling purchases as Needs wants savings and debts. You can be more detailed and categories like transport, food, and clothing. It all depends on an individual, how much weeds you want to get. After you have compiled everything in one list, get the total of every category to see how you spend. You will be shocked by the amount of money you spend on a particular expenditure.

Design a budget

When you track your spending, it will naturally lead to the next step: creating a budget. With the numbers you have from tracking your spending, you can now decide how much money you want to go into each item in your budget. You can also scale back some areas of your expenses that you discover you're overspending. You can write a budget as detailed as you like. Everybody's budget is different. Keep the budget relatively simple.

For proper budgeting, guideline uses the 50/30/20 rule — a strategy to help you divide and allocate your monthly income. The fifty percent will go towards fixed costs example, mortgage or rent, taxes, debt and car payments. The thirty percent will go towards spending, for example, vacation and eating out. And the 20% should go towards savings including emergency fund or investing. Regularly monitor your budget. It's better to start with a basic budget than not having a budget at all. Always save more than you're spending.

Set Financial Goals

Once you have attained your emergency savings account, you should work towards establishing financial goals. The financial goals can be short term goals such as holiday and long term goals such as saving for college, a house or a retirement plan. The mistakes most people make with their budget is they're short-sighted. Have a long term focus, have a five or ten-year plan. For example, it's easy to get money and buy that fancy car but, you can easily forget that you have a long term plan to have kids, and this can bring new expenses. Try to anticipate those long term goals and how to achieve them.

Set an Emergency Fund

You never know what the future will be. You could be unemployed or get an emergency. Whether you like it or not, life happens. Your emergency funding will be determined by your budget. Most financial expert's advice is saving 3 to 6 months' worth of expenses. Having an emergency fund to handle unplanned problem will help you feel more secured and prepared. Take away stressful emergencies with a financial cushion. Put your emergency fund in a savings account that is liquid and accessible, but only to be used for emergencies.

Apps Used for Money Management

Times are tough. Whether you earn a high net income or you get by, monitoring where your money is spent. There are many ways to track your spending, how you invest and more. We use our cell phones daily, and we always have our phones in our pockets all the time, using apps to help you manage your money is the best option.

Having a good understanding of your cash flow is very vital in managing your finances. How much of your income is coming in? When does the money get to your bank account? How do you spend the money? These are essential aspects of your financial success. Fortunately, there are a lot of money management apps in the market designed to help you check your bank balance, track your expenditure and, analyze your spending habits. Plus, there are apps that will assist you in making better financial decisions based on the data from your accounts.

And the best part? You can access your financial situation on the go. A lot of these money management apps can be checked online and also on your mobile device. It's very convenient as you can take care of your finances no matter where you are.

What do budget apps do? There are two main types of budget apps. One is an expense tracker — it best-fit people who deduct a lot of items from their taxes. For example, business owners who travel a lot, people who track their meals, transportation, and, all other professions who use expenses trackers. This app will help you track how much money you spend. You also have all the info you need when tax season rears its ugly head. The other type of budget app is the one which helps you track your bank budget, expenses bills, and utilities. These help you track your money, especially for people who manage multiple accounts and pays bills online.

Here are some of the best money management apps you should consider:

Personal Capital

Personal Capital has excellent features to track your budget and also include information about your investment accounts. And you can easily view on tablets, laptops, desktops and your mobile. It also shows graphs of your investments, that are easy to read and track down your investment performance.

Mint

Mint is one of the popular budgeting apps. Mint offer features like access to your investment accounts and budgeting tools. The budgeting portion is the main feature, and the investing part is little like an afterthought. The best app if you want to keep a very detailed budget. Mint also has a reminder feature to when your bills are due, and you can also pay your bills from the app.

Acorns

Acorns take virtual change out of your account. Instead of saving it, the app invests the difference. The app helps you start investing with virtually no effort. You can use Acorns on your transactions. The app has a new shopping type function, Found Money.

YNAB

YNAB is an acronym for You Need a Budget. YNAB cost $6.99 per month, but they waive the first month's fee. The philosophy for YNAB is " a job for every dollar." YNAB also offers a bank syncing and support feature. YNAB can also help you set your financial goals and make the most of each dollar earned.

Honeydue

Many couples use spreadsheets to manage their household finances. Honeydue is the best app for couples as it helps couples best co-manage their money. Honeydue helps to track shared bills; the pair can see their accounts in one spot, comment on the transactions, and build bigger and better financial goals. Honeydue has the main feature; couples can decide on how much they can share information with their significant others. This feature helps them to remain focused on their goals and not get caught in the weeds, arguing over the small stuff.

PocketGuard

PocketGuard will help you find savings in your spending. This app sync with your accounts and enables you to track and analyze your spending, which you can use that data to help you build an excellent budget. You can identify a pattern in your monthly spending, track your bills, and save some money.

Dollarbird

Dollarbird is an app that assists people who have issues with budgeting. This is a free app; however, it has premium add-ons. Your budget is put in a calendar form, and you can view any upcoming expenses. Other features are, you can color code transactions by category and pay you bills through the recurring transaction. Dollarbird lets you see the projected balance, so you are aware of how much money you can safely spend. The limitation that comes with this app is that the app does not sync with your bank account. With this app, you can quickly enter your transactions manually, and this means you will be more involved with the approach to your money.

Credit Karma

Credit Karma offers you access to your Credit Report. There are several uses of this app, for example, a company can use the app to determine whether to employ you or to estimate your credit score so as a business can be able to figure out the rates that they will charge you. This app can also be used to determine your loan applications and credit cards. Credit Karma is free to users however, the app earns money by offering targeted ads based on your credit score.

Chapter 13:
Risk Management Strategies

There is no guarantee in online trading. This means that even the best of traders will surely make losses at some point. This implies that it is vital for any trader to develop a good risk management strategy. The strategy adopted is as important as the trading strategy that they use. Mitigating your risks is surely one of the best ways of making sure you maintain your profits all through. In this case, a trader with a 50%-win rate could be more successful than a trader with a 75%-win rate and lacks a risk management strategy.

Traders should realize that two subsequent losses can tear away all the profits that had initially been accumulated. Therefore, it makes a lot of sense that you should have a risk management strategy which guarantees that you lock your profits and maximize returns. Simple strategies that could help you in securing your trading profits are discussed succinctly in this chapter.

Plan Your Trade

A fundamental step you need to take during trading is to plan your trade. Planning your trades is the surest way of knowing your chances of succeeding in any trade. By carefully planning your trade, you will find it easy to circumvent any challenges associated with day trading. Most traders will argue this out using the phrase "plan the trade and trade the plan[23]." If you are out to win, you basically should plan this out right before you enter any market.

How do you plan your trade? This begins by knowing that you are relying on the right trader. Not all brokers will be good for you. You need to rely on online reviews to find ideal brokers in the market. Ensure that you don't go for brokers who will charge you high commissions. The best brokers will offer you the best analytical tools to warrant that you know when to enter and exit the market.

You can also plan ahead by understanding how to use stop loss and take profit points. This implies that you will know when to take your profits and when to accept the losses you have already incurred. Failure to have a plan would only mean that you are gambling and not trading. With gambling, you could be lucky on unlucky. So, make sure that you plan your trade way before you enter the market.

One Percent Rule

A common way of mitigating your risks while trading is by following the one percent rule. This is a rule whereby a trader can only use about 1% of their trading capital. From what has been discussed, this applies mostly to traders who will be trading using large accounts. Assuming you have $10,000 as your trading capital, the one percent rule will require you to trade only $100. If you can afford to take more risks, you can use about 2% of your trading capital. The larger the account you use, the smaller the percentage you should risk. This is because the amount of money will increase. Keep your risks below 2%, and you will limit your losses.

Take Profit and Stop Loss Points

Take profit and stop loss points will undoubtedly help you in controlling your risks. Take profit point refers to the price where a trader sells their securities and takes home a certain amount of profit. Using take profit point warrants that a trader sells their securities for profit after enjoying a price increase for some time. It is always wise to know when to stop and close the trade.

There are instances where you will suffer losses following a fall in the price of your traded securities. When this happens, you should never forget to make use of stop loss points. Using these two points prevents you from adopting the mentality where you think the markets could turn around to your favor. It never does, and the chances are that sticking to the trade for long could only make you incur huge losses.

Diversify

Diversification will also be a smart strategy to adopt in guaranteeing that you reduce your risks. Investing all your capital in one security is the last thing that you should do. This will only put you at a higher risk of getting huge losses. Diversify your investments at all costs. The exciting aspect of diversification is that it opens doors to more opportunities to make a profit. This is because if one security fails to work, the other will compensate for the loss faced.

Hedging

Hedging goes hand in hand with diversification. Besides diversifying your securities, you need to hedge. Hedging could be understood as a form of insurance. When you hedge, you insure yourself against unforeseen losses. It should be noted that hedging will not prevent market prices from falling. However, it will prevent possible financial effects that could have been experienced. Therefore, when you hedge, the chances of making terrible losses are considerably reduced.

The idea of using hedging as a risk management strategy works in a similar manner like stop-loss tools. The main point of using these tools is to limit your losses as much as possible. There is a huge advantage gained when hedging is used carefully. For instance, you will make profits when you choose your second trade well.

A common misconception that traders have in mind with regards to hedging is that they need to make a similar trade to offset their first trade. Unfortunately, this is not how hedging is implemented as depicted in the image below.

Source: "Hedging Strategies – How to Trade Without ... - Trading Strategy Guides."[24]

It is only in forex trading that an individual could buy and sell simultaneously on similar pairs. In the event that there is a reversal in forex, hedging could come handy. Accordingly, when the market is rising and you find yourself short, you could choose to purchase temporarily to ensure that you hold a good position until the markets move in a way that favors you. This is explained well by the image below.

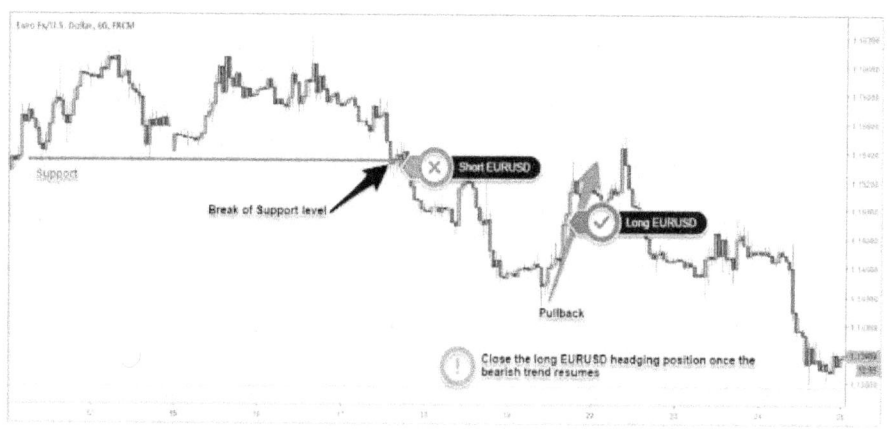

Source: "Hedging Strategies – How to Trade Without ... - Trading Strategy Guides.[25]"

After adopting a hedging strategy, a trader might end up thinking that since they are protected from possible losses, they can leave the trades to run for weeks. Well, it doesn't work that way. You need to bear in mind that there are carrying costs when using forex hedging. Hence, you can incur losses if you don't exit the trade in time.

There are different forms of hedging techniques which you could adopt. If you are thinking of using hedging to trade with a U.S. based forex trader, this is not possible. Nonetheless, there are tricks you could use to get around this. Usually, this is achieved through the idea of using multiple currencies. Notable hedging strategies you will come across in the market are as follows.

Gold Hedging Strategies

Inflation could easily affect the profits you make from your trades. Therefore, you need to hedge yourself from this occurrence by using gold. The benefit gain in using gold is that its price is maintained even when the dollar falls. The inverse correlation which exists between the U.S. dollar and gold will guarantee that you are protected. So, if the price of gold goes up, the price of the U.S. dollar will fall and vice versa.

Hedging Through Options

Hedging through options will also aid in safeguarding your trading portfolio. This strategy is best used when a trader sells put options and purchases call options. The advantage of using options is that they are regarded as the cheapest hedging option you can turn to.

In a word, traders should always find a way of managing their risks in any trading activity that they are involved in. Traders need to understand that they not only need to focus on making profits. Evidently, a high-profit margin can be canceled out by huge losses. Thus, managing losses is very crucial for the success of any trading activity.

Conclusion

As you can tell, after reading this book, there are many things to consider before you start trading more explicitly understanding the basics before moving on to more advanced techniques.

This book should have put you in a high position in terms of seeing results and achieving your goals. Keep in mind that for you to see amazing results, you will have to act on the information provided to you in this book since it will help you see results rather than daydreaming about it. The truth is that you can be making some serious cash flow within months if done correctly. Also, you need to make sure that whatever it is that you are doing is done with perfect calculations and at your own risk.

We can't stress enough how calculated you have to be with your investments, as it will only lead you to make more money. Finally, make sure that you not only take care of the investments by keeping track of it but also that you ease into every investment that you earn as it will only lead you to do make some smart decisions in the long run. Overall, I hope you learned a lot from this book. Most importantly, I hope you take a lot away from this book.

© Copyright 2020 - All rights reserved.

The content contained within this book may not be reproduced, duplicated or transmitted without direct written permission from the author or the publisher.

Under no circumstances will any blame or legal responsibility be held against the publisher, or author, for any damages, reparation, or monetary loss due to the information contained within this book. Either directly or indirectly.

Legal Notice:

This book is copyright protected. This book is only for personal use. You cannot amend, distribute, sell, use, quote or paraphrase any part, or the content within this book, without the consent of the author or publisher.

Disclaimer Notice:

Please note the information contained within this document is for educational and entertainment purposes only. All effort has been executed to present accurate, up to date, and reliable, complete information. No warranties of any kind are declared or implied. Readers acknowledge that the author is not engaging in the rendering of legal, financial, medical or professional advice. The content within this book has been derived from various sources. Please consult a licensed professional before attempting any techniques outlined in this book.

By reading this document, the reader agrees that under no circumstances is the author responsible for any losses, direct or indirect, which are incurred as a result of the use of information contained within this document, including, but not limited to, — errors, omissions, or inaccuracies.

www.ingramcontent.com/pod-product-compliance
Lightning Source LLC
Chambersburg PA
CBHW071407210526
45465CB00001B/286